Instant Pot®
FAMILY FAVORITES
COOKBOOK

pil

Publications International, Ltd.

Louis Weber, CEO
Publications International, Ltd.
8140 Lehigh Ave
Morton Grove, IL 60053

Pictured on the front cover *(top to bottom):* Pork Carnitas *(page 138)* and Southwestern Sloppy Joes *(page 108).*

Pictured on the back cover *(top to bottom):* Instant Spaghetti and Meatballs *(page 149)* and Perfect BBQ Ribs *(page 136).*

ISBN: 978-1-64558-896-2

Manufactured in China.

8 7 6 5 4 3 2 1

Instant Pot

CONTENTS

THE INDISPENSABLE Instant Pot®

Everyday cooking made simple

Preparing one, two or three meals a day can be exhausting, so let your Instant Pot—and the magic of pressure cooking—do the work for you. The recipes in this book were designed to minimize the time and energy you spend on cooking, with fewer steps and less cooking time than conventional recipes. But your family can still enjoy all their favorites, from chili mac and chocolate pudding cake to pot roast and potatoes—they'll just be quicker and easier to make than they used to be.

Penne with Ricotta, Tomatoes and Basil *(page 156)*

Why use a pressure cooker?

Speed is the main reason. In pressure cooking, liquid is heated in a heavy pot with a lid that locks and forms an airtight seal. Since the steam from the hot liquid is trapped inside and can't evaporate, the pressure increases and raises the boiling point of the contents in the pot, and these items cook faster at a higher temperature. In general, pressure cooking can reduce cooking time to about one third of the time used in conventional cooking methods—and typically the time spent on pressure cooking is hands off. (There's no peeking or stirring when food is being cooked under pressure.)

What makes the Instant Pot different?

The Instant Pot is a versatile electric multi-cooker that can be a pressure cooker, rice cooker, slow cooker, steamer and yogurt maker. The cooking programs you'll find on the control panel are convenient shortcuts for some foods you may prepare regularly (rice, beans, etc.) which use preset times and cooking levels. But in these pages we'll explore the basics of pressure cooking with recipes that use the Pressure Cook or Manual button along with customized cooking times and pressure levels. These simple and delicious dishes will inspire you to use your Instant Pot daily and create your own Instant Pot magic!

Instant Pot Components

The **exterior pot** is where the electrical components are housed. It should never be immersed in water; to clean it, simply unplug the unit, wipe it with a damp cloth and dry it immediately.

The **inner pot** holds the food and fits snugly into the exterior pot. Made of stainless steel, it is removable, and it can be washed by hand or in the dishwasher.

The **LED display** shows a time that indicates where the pressure cooker is in a particular function. The time counts down to zero from the number of minutes that were programmed. (The timing begins once the machine reaches pressure.) For Keep Warm and Yogurt functions, the time counts up.

The **pressure release valve** is on top of the lid and is used to seal the pot or release steam. To seal the pot, move the valve to the Sealing position; to release pressure, move the valve to the Venting position. This valve can pop off to clean, and to make sure nothing is blocking it.

The **float valve** controls the amount of pressure inside the pressure cooker and indicates when pressure cooking is taking place. The valve rises once the contents of the pot reach working pressure; it drops down when all the pressure has been released after cooking.

The **anti-block shield** is a small stainless steel cage found on the inside of the lid that prevents the pressure cooker from clogging. It can be removed for cleaning.

The **silicone sealing ring** underneath the lid helps create a tight seal to facilitate pressure cooking. The sealing ring has a tendency to absorb strong odors from cooking (particularly from acidic ingredients); washing it regularly with warm soapy water or in the dishwasher will help these odors dissipate, as will storing your Instant Pot with the lid ring side up. If you cook both sweet and savory dishes frequently, you may want to purchase an extra sealing ring (so the scent of curry or pot roast doesn't affect your rice pudding or crème brûlée). Make sure to inspect the ring before cooking—if it has any splits or cracks, it will not work properly and should be replaced.

Instant Pot Cooking Basics

Every recipe is slightly different, but most include these basic steps. Read through the entire recipe before beginning to cook so you'll know what ingredients to add and when to add them, which pressure level to use, the cooking time and the release method.

1. Sauté: Many recipes call for sautéing vegetables or browning meat at the beginning of a recipe to add flavor. (Be sure to leave the lid off in this step.)
2. Add the ingredients as the recipe directs and secure the lid, making sure the arrow mark on the lid is aligned with the "close" mark and lock icon on the rim of the outside pot. Turn the pressure release valve to the Sealing position.
3. Select Pressure Cook or Manual, then choose the pressure level. The default setting is high pressure, which is what most recipes in this book use. To change to low pressure, use the Pressure Level or Adjust button. To set the cooking time, use the + and - buttons. The Instant Pot will start automatically.
4. Once the pressure cooking is complete, use the pressure release method directed by the recipe. There are three types of releases:

Natural release:

Let the pressure slowly release on its own, which can take anywhere from 5 to 25 minutes (but is typically in the 10- to 15-minute range). The release time will be shorter for a pot that is less full and longer for one that is more full. When the float valve lowers, the pressure is released and you can open the lid.

Quick release:

Use a towel or pot holder to manually turn the pressure valve to the Venting position immediately after the cooking is complete. (Be sure to get out of the way of the steam before turning the valve.) It can take up to 2 minutes to fully release all the pressure; the float valve will drop down when all the pressure is released.

A combination of natural and quick release:

The recipe will instruct you to let the pressure release naturally for a certain amount of time (frequently for 10 minutes), and then do a quick release as directed.

Tips, Tricks, Dos and Don'ts

- Read the manual before beginning. There may be features you won't use, but it will eliminate some beginner's confusion, and it can help you understand how the Instant Pot works—and see all its possibilities. Models also change over time, so the manual can provide the best information about the buttons and functions of your pot. (Note that the terms "Pressure Cook" and "Manual" are interchangeable.)
- Don't overfill the pot—the total amount of food and liquid should not exceed the maximum level marked on the inner pot. Generally it is best not to fill the pot more than two thirds full; when cooking foods that expand during cooking such as beans and grains, do not fill it more than half full.
- Make sure there is always some liquid in the pot before cooking because a minimum amount is required to come up to pressure (the amount differs between models). However, if the recipe contains a large quantity of vegetables or meats, you may be able to use a bit less since these ingredients will create their own liquid.
- Always check that the pressure release valve is in the right position before you start pressure cooking. The food simply won't get cooked if the valve is not in the Sealing position because there will not be enough pressure in the pot.
- Never try to force the lid open after cooking—if the lid won't open, that means the pressure has not fully released. (As a safety feature, the lid remains locked until the float valve drops down.)
- Save the thickeners for after the pressure cooking is done. Pressure cooker recipes often end up with a lot of flavorful liquid left in the pot when cooking is complete; flour or cornstarch mixtures can thicken these liquids into delicious sauces. Use the Sauté function while incorporating the thickeners into the cooking liquid, and then cook and stir until the desired consistency is reached.
- Keep in mind that cooking times in some recipes may vary. We've included pressure cooking time charts as a guide (pages 184–187), but these are approximate times, and numerous variables may cause your results to be different. For example, the freshness of dried beans affects their cooking time (older beans take longer to cook), as does what they are cooked with—hard water (water that is high in mineral content), acidic ingredients, sugar and salt levels can also affect cooking times. So be flexible and experiment with what works best for you—you can always check the doneness of your food and add more time.
- Set reasonable expectations, i.e., don't expect everything you cook in the Instant Pot to be ready in a few minutes. Even though it reduces many conventional cooking times dramatically, nothing is literally "instant"—it will always take time to get up to pressure, and then to release it. (These machines are fast but not magical!)

Instant Pot®

BREAKFAST & BRUNCH

Shortcut Spanish Tortilla

MAKES 4 TO 6 SERVINGS

- 2 tablespoons olive oil
- 1 small onion, cut in half and thinly sliced
- 8 eggs
- ¼ teaspoon salt
- ⅛ teaspoon black pepper
- 4 ounces potato chips, lightly crushed (use plain thin chips, not kettle style)
- 1½ cups water
- Chopped fresh chives (optional)

1. Spray 7-inch metal cake pan with nonstick cooking spray. Press Sauté; heat oil in Instant Pot. Add onion; cook and stir about 4 minutes or until onion is softened and beginning to brown. Remove to small bowl; set aside to cool 5 minutes. Wipe out pot with paper towel.

2. Beat eggs, salt and pepper in medium bowl until blended. Add potato chips; fold in gently until all chips are coated. Let stand 5 minutes to soften. Stir in onion until well blended. Pour egg mixture into prepared pan; smooth top.

3. Pour water into pot; place rack in pot. Place pan on rack. Secure lid and move pressure release valve to Sealing position. Press Pressure Cook or Manual; cook at high pressure 20 minutes.

4. When cooking is complete, use quick release. Remove pan to wire rack; cool 5 minutes. Invert tortilla onto plate; invert again onto serving plate or cutting board. Garnish with chives; serve warm or at room temperature.

Pancake Breakfast Casserole

MAKES 6 SERVINGS

- **4 eggs**
- **1 cup half-and-half**
- **2 tablespoons sugar**
- **¾ teaspoon ground cinnamon, plus additional for garnish**
- **½ teaspoon vanilla**
- **9 frozen buttermilk pancakes (4-inch diameter), cut in half**
- **1 cup water**
- **Maple syrup**

1. Spray 1½-quart (6- to 7-inch) soufflé dish with nonstick cooking spray. Beat eggs, half-and-half, sugar, ¾ teaspoon cinnamon and vanilla in medium bowl until well blended.

2. Arrange 4 or 5 pancake halves standing up around side of prepared soufflé dish. Stack remaining pancake halves in soufflé dish, making layers as even as possible. Pour egg mixture over pancakes; press pancakes gently into liquid. Cover with foil; refrigerate overnight.

3. Remove soufflé dish from refrigerator at least 30 minutes before cooking. Pour water into Instant Pot; place rack in pot. Place soufflé dish on rack. Secure lid and move pressure release valve to Sealing position. Press Pressure Cook or Manual; cook at high pressure 30 minutes.

4. When cooking is complete, use natural release for 5 minutes, then release remaining pressure. Remove soufflé dish from pot. Uncover; sprinkle with additional cinnamon, if desired. Cut into wedges; serve warm with maple syrup.

Mini Broccoli Frittatas

MAKES 5 SERVINGS

- **1 broccoli crown (about 8 ounces)**
- **1 tablespoon olive oil**
- **1/3 cup chopped red onion**
- **1 cup plus 2 tablespoons water, divided**
- **3/4 teaspoon salt, divided**
- **1/4 cup diced roasted red pepper (1/4-inch pieces)**
- **Pinch red pepper flakes**
- **1/2 cup (2 ounces) crumbled goat cheese**
- **7 eggs**
- **3 tablespoons grated Parmesan or Asiago cheese**
- **3 tablespoons chopped fresh basil *or* 3/4 teaspoon dried basil**
- **2 tablespoons milk or water**
- **1/4 teaspoon black pepper**

1. Spray five 6-ounce ramekins or custard cups with nonstick cooking spray. Peel off tough outer skin of broccoli stem with paring knife; chop stem into 1/4-inch pieces. Chop top of broccoli into small florets (about 1/2 inch).

2. Press Sauté; heat oil in Instant Pot. Add onion; cook and stir 2 minutes. Add broccoli, 2 tablespoons water and 1/4 teaspoon salt; cook and stir about 5 minutes or until broccoli is crisp-tender. Add roasted pepper and red pepper flakes; cook and stir 1 minute. Remove vegetables to small bowl; stir in goat cheese. Wipe out pot with paper towel.

3. Beat eggs, Parmesan, basil, milk, remaining 1/2 teaspoon salt and black pepper in medium bowl until well blended. Divide vegetable mixture evenly among prepared ramekins; pour egg mixture over vegetables.

4. Pour remaining 1 cup water into pot; place rack in pot. Arrange ramekins on rack, stacking as necessary. Secure lid and move pressure release valve to Sealing position. Press Pressure Cook or Manual; cook at high pressure 17 minutes.

5. When cooking is complete, use quick release. Remove ramekins from pot; cool on wire rack 5 minutes. Serve frittatas warm in ramekins or turn out onto serving plates.

Lemon Blueberry Oatmeal

MAKES 4 SERVINGS

- **2 tablespoons butter**
- **1¼ cups steel-cut oats**
- **3¾ cups water**
- **½ teaspoon salt**
- **2 lemons**
- **4 tablespoons honey, divided**
- **¾ cup fresh blueberries**
- **½ cup chopped toasted almonds***

****To toast almonds, cook in small skillet over medium heat about 5 minutes or until lightly browned and fragrant, stirring frequently.***

1. Press Sauté; melt butter in Instant Pot. Add oats, cook about 6 minutes or until oats are browned and fragrant, stirring frequently. Stir in water and salt; mix well.

2. Secure lid and move pressure release valve to Sealing position. Press Pressure Cook or Manual; cook at high pressure 12 minutes.

3. Grate 4 teaspoons peel from lemons; squeeze 3 tablespoons juice.

4. When cooking is complete, use natural release for 10 minutes, then release remaining pressure. Stir oats until smooth. Add lemon juice, 2 teaspoons grated peel and 2 tablespoons honey; mix well.

5. Top each serving with blueberries, almonds and remaining lemon peel; drizzle with remaining honey.

Parmesan Garlic Monkey Bread

MAKES 6 TO 8 SERVINGS

- **2 tablespoons butter, melted**
- **2 tablespoons olive oil**
- **2 cloves garlic, minced**
- **1 teaspoon Italian seasoning**
- **¼ teaspoon salt**
- **1 cup grated Parmesan cheese (do not use shredded)**
- **1 container (about 16 ounces) refrigerated jumbo biscuits (8 biscuits)**
- **1 cup water**
- **Pizza sauce or marinara sauce (optional)**

1. Spray 6-cup bundt pan with nonstick cooking spray. Combine butter, oil, garlic, Italian seasoning and salt in medium bowl; mix well. Place cheese in shallow dish.

2. Separate biscuits; cut each biscuit into quarters. Dip each biscuit piece in butter mixture; roll in cheese to coat. Layer biscuit pieces in prepared pan; cover with foil.

3. Pour water into Instant Pot; place rack in pot. Place pan on rack. Secure lid and move pressure release valve to Sealing position. Press Pressure Cook or Manual; cook at high pressure 25 minutes. Preheat oven to 400°F. Line small baking sheet with foil; spray with cooking spray.

4. When cooking is complete, use natural release for 10 minutes, then release remaining pressure. Remove pan from pot. Uncover; let stand 10 minutes.

5. Invert monkey bread onto prepared baking sheet. Bake about 10 minutes or until top is golden brown. Serve with pizza sauce for dipping, if desired.

Crustless Spinach Quiche

MAKES 6 SERVINGS

- 6 eggs
- ¾ cup half-and-half
- ¾ teaspoon Italian seasoning
- ½ teaspoon salt
- ½ teaspoon black pepper
- 1 package (10 ounces) frozen chopped spinach, thawed and squeezed dry
- 1 cup (4 ounces) shredded Italian cheese blend
- 1½ cups water

1. Spray 7-inch metal cake pan with nonstick cooking spray. Beat eggs, half-and-half, Italian seasoning, salt and pepper in medium bowl until well blended. Stir in spinach and cheese; mix well. Pour into prepared pan; cover with foil.

2. Pour water into Instant Pot; place rack in pot. Place pan on rack. Secure lid and move pressure release valve to Sealing position. Press Pressure Cook or Manual; cook at high pressure 28 minutes.

3. When cooking is complete, use natural release for 5 minutes, then release remaining pressure. Remove pan from pot. Uncover; let stand 5 minutes before serving.

Tip

To remove the quiche from the pan for serving, run a knife around the edge of the pan to loosen. Invert the quiche onto a plate; invert again onto a cutting board or serving plate. Cut into wedges to serve.

French Toast Casserole

MAKES 6 SERVINGS

- **1 loaf (14 to 16 ounces) day-old cinnamon swirl bread (see Tip)**
- **4 ounces cream cheese, cubed**
- **1½ cups whole milk**
- **4 eggs**
- **¼ cup maple syrup, plus additional for serving**
- **⅛ teaspoon salt**
- **1 cup water**

1. Spray 1½-quart (6- to 7-inch) soufflé dish with nonstick cooking spray. Cut bread into 1-inch pieces. (You should have 5 to 6 cups bread cubes.) Place one third of bread in prepared soufflé dish; top with half of cream cheese cubes. Repeat layers; top with remaining bread.

2. Whisk milk, eggs, ¼ cup maple syrup and salt in medium bowl until well blended. Pour over bread and cream cheese; press gently into liquid. Cover with foil; let stand 30 minutes.

3. Pour water into Instant Pot; place rack in pot. Place soufflé dish on rack. Secure lid and move pressure release valve to Sealing position. Press Pressure Cook or Manual; cook at high pressure 35 minutes.

4. When cooking is complete, use natural release for 5 minutes, then release remaining pressure. Remove soufflé dish from pot. Uncover; let stand 5 minutes before serving. Cut into wedges; serve warm with additional maple syrup.

Tip

Day-old bread is drier than fresh bread and better able to absorb the custard mixture in casseroles and bread puddings. If you only have fresh bread, bake the bread cubes on a baking sheet in a 350°F oven about 7 minutes or until lightly toasted.

Big Denver Omelet

MAKES 8 SERVINGS

- 1 tablespoon butter
- 1/3 cup chopped onion
- 1/3 cup diced red bell pepper (1/4-inch pieces)
- 1/3 cup diced green bell pepper (1/4-inch pieces)
- 1/3 cup diced ham (1/4-inch pieces)
- 8 eggs
- 2 tablespoons milk
- 1/2 teaspoon salt
- 1/4 teaspoon black pepper
- 1/2 cup (2 ounces) shredded Cheddar cheese
- 1 1/2 cups water

1. Press Sauté; melt butter in Instant Pot. Add onion, bell peppers and ham; cook and stir about 3 minutes or until vegetables begin to soften. Remove to plate to cool slightly. Wipe out pot with paper towel.

2. Spray 6-cup nonstick bundt pan generously with nonstick cooking spray. (Make sure crevices and bottom of pan are very well greased to prevent sticking.) Beat eggs, milk, salt and black pepper in medium bowl until blended. Stir in cheese and vegetable mixture; mix well. Pour into prepared pan. Cover with foil.

3. Pour water into pot; place rack in pot. Place pan on rack. Secure lid and move pressure release valve to Sealing position. Press Pressure Cook or Manual; cook at high pressure 14 minutes.

4. When cooking is complete, use natural release for 5 minutes, then release remaining pressure. Remove pan from pot. Uncover; blot any condensation on top of omelet with paper towel. Cool in pan on wire rack 10 minutes. Loosen edges and bottom of omelet with knife or narrow spatula before inverting omelet onto plate. Invert again onto serving plate (so more attractive side faces up). Serve warm.

Instant Pot

BEANS & GRAINS

Greek Giant Beans in Tomato Sauce

MAKES ABOUT 8 SERVINGS

- 1 pound dried gigante beans* (about 2¼ cups)
- 1½ tablespoons salt, divided
- 2 bay leaves
- ¼ cup olive oil
- 2 small onions, chopped
- 1 stalk celery, finely chopped
- 1 medium carrot, finely chopped
- 3 cloves garlic, minced
- 1 teaspoon dried oregano, plus additional for serving
- ⅛ teaspoon red pepper flakes
- 1 can (28 ounces) whole tomatoes, undrained, coarsely chopped or crushed with hands
- 2 tablespoons tomato paste
- ½ teaspoon black pepper
- Chopped fresh parsley
- Crumbled feta cheese

**If gigante beans are not available, use another variety of large white beans such as lima, butter or corona beans.*

1. Rinse, drain and sort beans. Combine beans, 8 cups water and 1 tablespoon salt in medium bowl; soak 8 hours or overnight.

2. Drain beans; add to Instant Pot with 6 cups water and bay leaves. Secure lid and move pressure release valve to Sealing position. Press Pressure Cook or Manual; cook at high pressure 15 minutes. When cooking is complete, use natural release for 20 minutes, then release remaining pressure. Drain beans in colander, reserving 1 cup cooking liquid. Wipe out pot with paper towel.

3. Press Sauté; heat oil in pot. Add onions, celery and carrot; cook and stir 5 minutes or until vegetables are softened. Add garlic, 1 teaspoon oregano and red pepper flakes; cook and stir 30 seconds. Add tomatoes with liquid, tomato paste, remaining ½ tablespoon salt and black pepper; mix well. Stir in beans and ⅓ cup bean cooking liquid.

4. Secure lid and move pressure release valve to Sealing position. Press Pressure Cook or Manual; cook at high pressure 5 minutes.

5. When cooking is complete, use natural release for 10 minutes, then release remaining pressure. If sauce is too thin, press Sauté; cook 5 minutes until slightly thickened and reduced, stirring frequently. If sauce is too thick, stir in additional bean cooking liquid. Top with parsley, cheese and additional oregano.

Peasant Risotto

MAKES 4 SERVINGS

- 2 tablespoons olive oil, divided
- 3 ounces prosciutto or ham, chopped
- 1/4 cup chopped green onions
- 2 cloves garlic, minced
- 1/2 teaspoon dried sage
- 1 cup uncooked arborio rice
- 2 3/4 cups chicken broth
- 1 can (about 15 ounces) Great Northern beans, rinsed and drained
- 1/4 teaspoon salt
- 1 1/2 cups packed stemmed shredded Swiss chard
- 1/2 cup grated Parmesan cheese

1. Press Sauté; heat 1 tablespoon oil in Instant Pot. Add prosciutto; cook and stir 3 minutes. Add green onions, garlic and sage; cook and stir 1 minute. Add remaining 1 tablespoon oil and rice; cook and stir 2 minutes or until rice is translucent. Stir in broth, beans and salt; mix well.

2. Secure lid and move pressure release valve to Sealing position. Press Pressure Cook or Manual; cook at high pressure 6 minutes.

3. When cooking is complete, use quick release. Press Sauté; add Swiss chard to pot. Cook and stir 3 minutes or until Swiss chard is wilted. Stir in cheese. Serve immediately.

Pumpkin Black Bean Soup

MAKES 6 TO 8 SERVINGS

- 1 tablespoon olive oil
- 6 green onions, cut into ¼-inch slices, divided
- 1 red bell pepper, diced
- 2 cloves garlic, minced
- 1 teaspoon ground cumin
- 1 teaspoon smoked paprika
- ¼ teaspoon black pepper
- 2 cans (about 15 ounces each) black beans, rinsed and drained
- 2 cups vegetable broth or water
- 1 can (15 ounces) pure pumpkin
- 1 can (about 14 ounces) diced tomatoes
- 1 teaspoon salt
- Juice of 1 lime

1. Press Sauté; heat oil in Instant Pot. Reserve 1 green onion for garnish. Add remaining 5 green onions and bell pepper to pot; cook and stir 2 minutes. Add garlic, cumin, paprika and black pepper; cook and stir 1 minute. Stir in beans, broth, pumpkin, tomatoes and salt; mix well.

2. Secure lid and move pressure release valve to Sealing position. Press Pressure Cook or Manual; cook at high pressure 8 minutes.

3. When cooking is complete, use natural release for 10 minutes, then release remaining pressure. Stir in lime juice; top with reserved green onion.

Classic Hummus

MAKES ABOUT 3¼ CUPS

- 4 cups water
- 8 ounces dried chickpeas, rinsed and sorted
- 1½ teaspoons salt, divided
- ¼ cup lemon juice
- 2 cloves garlic, minced
- ¼ teaspoon ground cumin
- ½ cup tahini
- 2 tablespoons extra virgin olive oil, plus additional for serving
- Chopped fresh parsley (optional)
- Paprika or za'atar (optional)

1. Combine water, chickpeas and 1 teaspoon salt in Instant Pot; mix well. Secure lid and move pressure release valve to Sealing position. Press Pressure Cook or Manual; cook at high pressure 45 minutes.

2. When cooking is complete, use natural release. Drain chickpeas, reserving 1 cup cooking liquid.

3. Combine lemon juice, garlic, remaining ½ teaspoon salt and cumin in bowl of food processor; let stand 5 minutes. Add tahini and ¼ cup cooking liquid; process until well blended. Add cooked chickpeas, 2 tablespoons oil and ⅓ cup cooking liquid; process about 3 minutes or until very smooth, stopping to scrape down side of bowl once or twice. Add additional cooking liquid, 1 tablespoon at a time, if necessary to thin hummus.

4. Top hummus with additional oil, parsley and paprika, if desired.

Black Beans and Rice

MAKES 6 TO 8 SERVINGS

- 1 tablespoon vegetable oil
- 1 onion, chopped
- 1 cup uncooked long grain rice, rinsed well and drained
- 3/4 cup plus 2 tablespoons water
- 3/4 cup chunky salsa, divided
- 4 teaspoons taco seasoning mix, divided
- 1/2 teaspoon salt
- 1 can (about 15 ounces) black beans, rinsed and drained

1. Press Sauté; heat oil in Instant Pot. Add onion; cook and stir 3 minutes or until softened. Add rice, water, 1/4 cup salsa, 1 teaspoon taco seasoning and salt; mix well.

2. Secure lid and move pressure release valve to Sealing position. Press Pressure Cook or Manual; cook at high pressure 5 minutes.

3. When cooking is complete, use natural release for 10 minutes, then release remaining pressure. Stir rice.

4. Press Sauté; adjust heat to low. Add beans, remaining 1/2 cup salsa and 1 tablespoon taco seasoning; cook and stir about 3 minutes or until heated through.

Shortcut Baked Beans

MAKES 6 TO 8 SERVINGS

- **5 slices thick-cut bacon, chopped**
- **1 small onion, chopped**
- **3½ cups water**
- **1 pound dried pinto beans, rinsed and sorted**
- **1 cup barbecue sauce**
- **¼ cup ketchup**
- **½ teaspoon salt**

1. Press Sauté; cook bacon in Instant Pot until crisp. Drain off all but 1 tablespoon drippings.

2. Add onion to pot; cook and stir 3 minutes or until softened. Add water and beans; cook 1 minute, scraping up browned bits from bottom of pot. Stir in barbecue sauce and ketchup; mix well.

3. Secure lid and move pressure release valve to Sealing position. Press Pressure Cook or Manual; cook at high pressure 50 minutes.

4. When cooking is complete, use natural release for 15 minutes, then release remaining pressure. Stir beans; season with salt. If there is excess liquid in pot, press Sauté and cook 3 to 5 minutes or until liquid is reduced, stirring frequently.

Farro with Butternut Squash and Kale

MAKES 6 TO 8 SERVINGS

- 2 tablespoons olive oil
- 1 small red onion, chopped
- 2 cloves garlic, minced
- ½ teaspoon dried thyme
- 1½ cups uncooked farro, rinsed and drained
- 2 cups vegetable broth
- 1½ teaspoons salt
- ¼ teaspoon black pepper
- 1 small butternut squash (about 1½ pounds), peeled and cut into ¾-inch pieces (3 cups)
- 1 small bunch lacinato kale, stemmed and cut crosswise into 1-inch-wide strips (3 cups)
- ½ cup grated Parmesan cheese

1. Press Sauté; heat oil in Instant Pot. Add onion; cook and stir 3 minutes or until softened. Add garlic and thyme; cook and stir 1 minute. Add farro; cook and stir 2 minutes. Stir in broth, salt and pepper; mix well.

2. Secure lid and move pressure release valve to Sealing position. Press Pressure Cook or Manual; cook at high pressure 7 minutes.

3. When cooking is complete, use quick release. Stir in squash and kale. Secure lid and move pressure release valve to Sealing position. Press Pressure Cook or Manual; cook at high pressure 3 minutes.

4. When cooking is complete, use natural release for 5 minutes, then release remaining pressure. Stir in cheese.

Mexican-Style Charro Beans

MAKES 8 SERVINGS

- 1 pound dried pinto beans, soaked 8 hours or overnight
- 4 slices thick-cut bacon, chopped
- 1 white onion, chopped
- 1 jalapeño pepper, seeded and finely chopped
- 3 cloves garlic, minced
- 1½ teaspoons salt
- 1½ teaspoons chili powder
- 1½ teaspoons ground cumin
- 1 teaspoon dried oregano
- ½ teaspoon black pepper
- 3 cups chicken broth
- 1 can (about 14 ounces) diced fire-roasted tomatoes
- 2 bay leaves

1. Drain and rinse beans. Press Sauté; cook bacon in Instant Pot until crisp. Remove to paper towel-lined plate. Drain off all but 1 tablespoon drippings.

2. Add onion and jalapeño to pot; cook and stir 3 minutes or until softened. Add garlic; cook and stir 1 minute. Add salt, chili powder, cumin, oregano and black pepper; cook and stir 30 seconds. Stir in beans, broth, tomatoes, bacon and bay leaves; mix well.

3. Secure lid and move pressure release valve to Sealing position. Press Pressure Cook or Manual; cook at high pressure 25 minutes.

4. When cooking is complete, use natural release. Remove and discard bay leaves. Stir beans; add additional salt to taste.

Jalapeño Cheddar Corn Bread

MAKES 8 SERVINGS

- **1 cup yellow cornmeal**
- **¾ cup all-purpose flour**
- **⅓ cup sugar**
- **2 teaspoons baking powder**
- **1 teaspoon salt**
- **1 cup buttermilk or whole milk**
- **2 eggs**
- **3 tablespoons butter, melted**
- **1 cup (4 ounces) shredded Cheddar cheese**
- **2 jalapeño peppers, seeded and minced (about ⅓ cup)**
- **1½ cups water**

1. Spray 7-inch springform pan with nonstick cooking spray. Combine cornmeal, flour, sugar, baking powder and salt in large bowl; mix well.

2. Beat buttermilk, eggs and butter in medium bowl until blended. Add to cornmeal mixture; stir just until blended. Stir in cheese and jalapeños until blended. Spread batter evenly in prepared pan; cover with foil.

3. Pour water into Instant Pot; place rack in pot. Place pan on rack. Secure lid and move pressure release valve to Sealing position. Press Pressure Cook or Manual; cook at high pressure 30 minutes.

4. When cooking is complete, use quick release. Remove pan from pot. Uncover; cool on wire rack 5 minutes before serving.

Vegetarian Quinoa Chili

MAKES 4 TO 6 SERVINGS

- 2 tablespoons vegetable oil
- 1 large onion, chopped
- 1 red bell pepper, chopped
- 1 large carrot, diced
- 1 stalk celery, diced
- 1 jalapeño pepper, seeded and finely chopped
- 1 tablespoon minced garlic
- 1 tablespoon chili powder
- 2 teaspoons ground cumin
- 1 teaspoon salt
- 1 can (28 ounces) crushed tomatoes
- 1 can (about 15 ounces) kidney beans, rinsed and drained
- 3/4 cup water
- 1/2 cup uncooked quinoa, rinsed well and drained
- 1 cup fresh or frozen corn
- Optional toppings: diced avocado, shredded Cheddar cheese and/or sliced green onions

1. Press Sauté; heat oil in Instant Pot. Add onion, bell pepper, carrot and celery; cook 5 minutes or until vegetables are softened, stirring occasionally. Add jalapeño, garlic, chili powder, cumin and salt; cook and stir 1 minute or until fragrant. Add tomatoes, beans, water and quinoa; mix well.

2. Secure lid and move pressure release valve to Sealing position. Press Pressure Cook or Manual; cook at high pressure 8 minutes.

3. When cooking is complete, use quick release. Stir in corn; cover and let stand 2 minutes or until corn is heated through. Serve with desired toppings.

Greek White Bean Soup

MAKES 4 TO 6 SERVINGS

- **1 package (16 ounces) dried cannellini or Great Northern beans, soaked 8 hours or overnight**
- **4 tablespoons olive oil, divided**
- **1 large onion, diced**
- **3 stalks celery, diced**
- **3 carrots, diced**
- **4 cloves garlic, minced**
- **¼ cup tomato paste**
- **1 teaspoon salt**
- **1 teaspoon dried oregano**
- **½ teaspoon ground cumin**
- **¼ teaspoon black pepper**
- **1 bay leaf**
- **1 container (32 ounces) vegetable broth**
- **½ cup water**
- **2 tablespoons lemon juice**
- **¼ cup minced fresh parsley**

1. Drain and rinse beans. Press Sauté; heat 2 tablespoons oil in Instant Pot. Add onion, celery and carrots; cook and stir 8 to 10 minutes or until vegetables are softened. Add garlic; cook and stir 30 seconds. Add tomato paste, salt, oregano, cumin, pepper and bay leaf; cook and stir 30 seconds. Stir in broth, water and beans; mix well.

2. Secure lid and move pressure release valve to Sealing position. Press Pressure Cook or Manual; cook at high pressure 10 minutes.

3. When cooking is complete, use natural release for 10 minutes, then release remaining pressure. Remove and discard bay leaf. Stir in remaining 2 tablespoons oil and lemon juice. Sprinkle with parsley just before serving.

Instant Pot PASTA

Orchiette with Sausage and Broccoli Rabe

MAKES 4 TO 6 SERVINGS

- **1 tablespoon olive oil**
- **12 ounces bulk mild Italian sausage**
- **1 bunch broccoli rabe (about 1 pound), tough stems removed, cut into 2-inch-long pieces**
- **3 cloves garlic, minced**
- **¼ teaspoon red pepper flakes**
- **¼ cup dry white wine**
- **1 package (16 ounces) uncooked orchiette pasta**
- **4 cups chicken broth**
- **⅓ cup water**
- **1 teaspoon salt**
- **¾ cup grated Parmesan cheese, divided**
- **Juice of 1 lemon**

1. Press Sauté; heat oil in Instant Pot. Add sausage; cook about 8 minutes or until browned, stirring to break up meat. Remove to plate with slotted spoon. Add broccoli rabe to pot; cook and stir 5 minutes or until crisp-tender. Remove to serving bowl; cover with foil to keep warm.

2. Return sausage to pot. Add garlic and red pepper flakes; cook and stir 1 minute. Add wine; cook 2 minutes, scraping up browned bits from bottom of pot. Stir in pasta, broth, water and salt; mix well, separating pasta pieces as much as possible. (Orchiette often sticks together in stacks in the package and during cooking.)

3. Secure lid and move pressure release valve to Sealing position. Press Pressure Cook or Manual; cook at high pressure 5 minutes.

4. When cooking is complete, use quick release. Stir in broccoli rabe, ½ cup cheese and lemon juice; mix well. Serve immediately with remaining cheese.

Turkey Vegetable Chili Mac

MAKES 6 SERVINGS

- 1 tablespoon vegetable oil
- 1 pound ground turkey
- 1 cup chopped onion
- 2 cloves garlic, minced
- 1 can (about 15 ounces) black beans, rinsed and drained
- 1 can (about 14 ounces) diced tomatoes with onion and bell pepper
- 1 can (about 14 ounces) diced tomatoes
- 1½ cups water
- 1 cup uncooked elbow macaroni
- 1 teaspoon salt
- 1 teaspoon chili powder
- ½ teaspoon ground cumin
- 1 cup frozen corn
- Sour cream (optional)
- Chopped fresh parsley or cilantro (optional)

1. Press Sauté; heat oil in Instant Pot. Add turkey, onion and garlic; cook and stir 5 minutes or until turkey is no longer pink. Stir in beans, tomatoes, water, macaroni, salt, chili powder and cumin; mix well.

2. Secure lid and move pressure release valve to Sealing position. Press Pressure Cook or Manual; cook at high pressure 3 minutes.

3. When cooking is complete, use quick release. Press Sauté; add corn to pot. Cook about 2 minutes or until corn is heated through and any excess liquid is absorbed, stirring occasionally. Garnish with sour cream and parsley.

Easy Cheesy Lasagna

MAKES 4 TO 6 SERVINGS

- 1 cup ricotta cheese
- 1¾ cups (7 ounces) shredded Italian blend cheese, divided
- 1 egg
- 2 cups pasta sauce
- 8 no-boil lasagna noodles (about 5 ounces)
- 1½ cups water

1. Spray 7-inch springform pan with nonstick cooking spray. Beat ricotta, ½ cup shredded cheese and egg in small bowl until well blended.

2. Spread ½ cup pasta sauce on bottom of prepared pan. Top with 2 noodles, breaking to fit and cover sauce layer. Spread one third of ricotta mixture over sauce; top with ¼ cup shredded cheese. Repeat layers of sauce, noodles, ricotta mixture and shredded cheese twice, pressing down gently. Top with remaining 2 noodles, ½ cup pasta sauce and ½ cup shredded cheese. Cover pan with foil sprayed with nonstick cooking spray (or use nonstick foil).

3. Pour water into Instant Pot; place rack in pot. Place pan on rack. Secure lid and move pressure release valve to Sealing position. Press Pressure Cook or Manual; cook at high pressure 16 minutes. Preheat broiler.

4. When cooking is complete, use natural release for 5 minutes, then release remaining pressure. Remove pan from pot. Uncover; place lasagna on baking sheet. Broil about 3 minutes or until top is golden brown in spots.

Classic Macaroni and Cheese

MAKES 4 TO 6 SERVINGS

- 2 cups uncooked elbow macaroni
- 2 cups water
- 1½ teaspoons salt, divided
- 1 can (5 ounces) evaporated milk
- 3 cups (12 ounces) shredded Colby-Jack cheese*
- ⅛ teaspoon black pepper

**Or substitute 6 ounces each shredded Colby and Monterey Jack cheeses.*

1. Combine macaroni, water and 1 teaspoon salt in Instant Pot; mix well. Secure lid and move pressure release valve to Sealing position. Press Pressure Cook or Manual; cook at high pressure 4 minutes.

2. When cooking is complete, use quick release. Press Sauté; alternately add milk and handfuls of cheese to pot, stirring constantly until cheese is melted and smooth. Stir in remaining ½ teaspoon salt and pepper.

Chicken with Parmesan Fettuccine

MAKES 4 SERVINGS

- **1 pound boneless skinless chicken breasts, cut into bite-size pieces**
- **1 teaspoon salt, divided**
- **¼ teaspoon black pepper**
- **2 tablespoons butter, divided**
- **1 clove garlic, minced**
- **1½ cups chicken broth**
- **8 ounces uncooked fettuccine, broken in half**
- **⅔ cup whipping cream**
- **½ cup grated Parmesan cheese**
- **½ cup chopped green onions**

1. Season chicken with ½ teaspoon salt and pepper. Press Sauté; melt 1 tablespoon butter in Instant Pot. Add chicken and garlic; cook 5 minutes without stirring. Cook and stir 1 minute; remove to medium bowl. Add broth to pot; cook 1 minute, scraping up browned bits from bottom of pot.

2. Add pasta and remaining ½ teaspoon salt to pot, pressing pasta down into broth. Top with chicken. (Do not stir.)

3. Secure lid and move pressure release valve to Sealing position. Press Pressure Cook or Manual; cook at high pressure 5 minutes.

4. When cooking is complete, use quick release. Add cream and remaining 1 tablespoon butter to pot; cook and stir 3 to 4 minutes or until pasta is al dente and most of liquid is absorbed. Gradually add cheese, stirring until blended. Stir in green onions.

Asian Chicken and Noodles

MAKES 4 SERVINGS

- 1 tablespoon vegetable oil
- 1 pound boneless skinless chicken breasts, cut into 1×½-inch pieces
- 1 bottle or jar (about 12 ounces) stir-fry sauce
- ¾ cup chicken broth or water
- 8 ounces uncooked thin Pad Thai rice noodles (⅛ inch wide)
- 1 package (16 ounces) frozen stir-fry vegetable blend (do not thaw)

1. Press Sauté; heat oil in Instant Pot. Add chicken; cook about 4 minutes or until no longer pink, stirring occasionally.

2. Stir in stir-fry sauce and broth; mix well. Top with noodles, breaking to fit as necessary. Cover with vegetables in even layer. (Do not stir.)

3. Secure lid and move pressure release valve to Sealing position. Press Pressure Cook or Manual; cook at high pressure 2 minutes.

4. When cooking is complete, use quick release. Stir with tongs to separate noodles and coat noodles and vegetables with sauce. If there is excess liquid in pot, press Sauté; cook and stir 2 minutes or until liquid has evaporated.

Penne with Chunky Tomato Sauce and Spinach

MAKES 4 SERVINGS

- 1 tablespoon olive oil
- 1 cup chopped onion
- 2 cloves garlic, minced
- 2 teaspoons salt
- ½ teaspoon dried oregano
- ½ teaspoon dried basil
- ¼ teaspoon red pepper flakes
- ¼ teaspoon black pepper
- 1 can (6 ounces) tomato paste
- 2 cups water
- 8 ounces uncooked penne pasta
- 1 package (5 ounces) baby spinach
- 1 large ripe tomato, seeded and chopped
- ¼ cup grated Parmesan cheese
- ¼ cup chopped fresh basil

1. Press Sauté; heat oil in Instant Pot. Add onion and garlic; cook and stir 3 minutes or until onion is softened. Add salt, oregano, dried basil, red pepper flakes and black pepper; cook and stir 30 seconds. Add tomato paste; cook and stir 1 minute. Add water; stir until well blended. Stir in pasta; mix well.

2. Secure lid and move pressure release valve to Sealing position. Press Pressure Cook or Manual; cook at high pressure 4 minutes.

3. When cooking is complete, use quick release. Stir in spinach and tomato; cover and let stand 2 to 3 minutes or until spinach is wilted. Top with cheese and fresh basil.

Chili Spaghetti Supper

MAKES 4 TO 6 SERVINGS

- 1 pound lean ground beef
- 1 medium onion, chopped
- 1 teaspoon salt
- 1/4 teaspoon black pepper
- 1 can (about 15 ounces) chili beans in mild sauce
- 1 can (about 14 ounces) Italian-seasoned diced tomatoes
- 2 teaspoons chili powder
- 1/4 teaspoon garlic powder
- 8 ounces uncooked spaghetti
- 1/2 cup water
- 1 1/2 cups (6 ounces) shredded sharp Cheddar cheese, divided
- 1/4 cup sour cream

1. Press Sauté; add beef, onion, salt and pepper to Instant Pot. Cook about 8 minutes or until beef is no longer pink, stirring to break up meat. Drain fat.

2. Stir in beans, tomatoes, chili powder and garlic powder; mix well. Break spaghetti in half; add to pot with water.

3. Secure lid and move pressure release valve to Sealing position. Press Pressure Cook or Manual; cook at high pressure 5 minutes.

4. When cooking is complete, use quick release. Press Sauté; stir in 1 cup cheese and sour cream. Cook and stir 1 minute or until cheese is melted and mixture is well blended. Turn off heat; cover and let stand 3 minutes or until excess liquid is absorbed and pasta is tender. Sprinkle with remaining 1/2 cup cheese.

Instant Pot VEGETABLES

Quick-Cooking Ratatouille

MAKES ABOUT 6 CUPS

- **2 tablespoons extra virgin olive oil**
- **1 medium onion, chopped**
- **2 red bell peppers, cut into 1-inch pieces**
- **3 cloves garlic, minced**
- **1 teaspoon Italian seasoning**
- **Pinch red pepper flakes**
- **1 can (28 ounces) whole tomatoes, undrained, coarsely chopped or crushed with hands**
- **1 medium eggplant (about 1 pound), cut into ½-inch pieces**
- **3 small zucchini (about 12 ounces), cut in half lengthwise and cut crosswise into ¾-inch slices**
- **1 large sprig fresh basil**
- **1 tablespoon tomato paste**
- **1½ teaspoons salt**
- **¼ teaspoon black pepper**
- **1 tablespoon balsamic or red wine vinegar**
- **¼ cup chopped fresh basil**

1. Press Sauté; heat oil in Instant Pot. Add onion; cook and stir 2 minutes. Add bell peppers; cook and stir 3 minutes. Add garlic, Italian seasoning and red pepper flakes; cook and stir 30 seconds. Stir in tomatoes with liquid, eggplant, zucchini, basil sprig, tomato paste, salt and black pepper; mix well.

2. Secure lid and move pressure release valve to Sealing position. Press Pressure Cook or Manual; cook at high pressure 1 minute.

3. When cooking is complete, use quick release. Press Sauté; cook about 5 minutes or until slightly thickened. Remove and discard basil sprig. Stir in vinegar and chopped basil. Serve warm or at room temperature.

Mediterranean Red Potatoes

MAKES 4 TO 6 SERVINGS

- **2 pounds unpeeled red potatoes, cut into 1-inch pieces**
- **1 cup frozen pearl onions *or* 1 large onion, cut into 1-inch pieces**
- **1 cup water**
- **2 tablespoons extra virgin olive oil, divided**
- **1 teaspoon salt**
- **1 teaspoon Italian seasoning**
- **½ teaspoon garlic powder**
- **¼ teaspoon black pepper**
- **1 small tomato, seeded and chopped**
- **½ cup crumbled feta cheese**
- **2 tablespoons chopped black olives**

1. Combine potatoes, onions, water, 1 tablespoon oil, salt, Italian seasoning, garlic powder and pepper in Instant Pot; mix well.

2. Secure lid and move pressure release valve to Sealing position. Press Pressure Cook or Manual; cook at high pressure 3 minutes.

3. When cooking is complete, use quick release. Drain excess liquid from pot.

4. Add remaining 1 tablespoon oil, tomato, cheese and olives to potatoes; stir gently to blend.

Thai-Style Butternut Squash

MAKES 4 TO 6 SERVINGS

- 1/3 cup flaked coconut
- 2 teaspoons vegetable oil
- 1/2 small onion *or* 1 shallot, finely chopped
- 2 cloves garlic, minced
- 1 cup unsweetened coconut milk
- 1/4 cup packed brown sugar
- 1 tablespoon fish sauce or soy sauce
- 1/2 teaspoon salt
- 1/8 teaspoon red pepper flakes
- 1 butternut squash (2 to 2½ pounds), peeled and cut into 3/4-inch cubes
- 1 tablespoon chopped fresh cilantro

1. Preheat oven to 350°F. Spread coconut in baking pan. Bake 6 minutes or until golden brown, stirring occasionally. Set aside to cool and crisp.

2. Press Sauté; heat oil in Instant Pot. Add onion and garlic; cook and stir 3 minutes or until onion is softened. Add coconut milk, brown sugar, fish sauce, salt and red pepper flakes; stir until brown sugar is dissolved. Stir in squash; mix well.

3. Secure lid and move pressure release valve to Sealing position. Press Pressure Cook or Manual; cook at high pressure 1 minute.

4. When cooking is complete, use quick release. Remove squash to serving bowl with slotted spoon.

5. Press Sauté; cook sauce about 2 minutes or until thickened. Pour sauce over squash; stir gently to blend. Sprinkle with toasted coconut and cilantro.

Chunky Ranch Potatoes

MAKES 8 SERVINGS

- 3 pounds unpeeled red potatoes, quartered
- ½ cup water
- 1 teaspoon salt
- ½ cup ranch dressing
- ½ cup grated Parmesan cheese
- ¼ cup minced fresh chives

1. Combine potatoes, water and salt in Instant Pot; mix well.

2. Secure lid and move pressure release valve to Sealing position. Press Pressure Cook or Manual; cook at high pressure 5 minutes.

3. When cooking is complete, use quick release. Add ranch dressing, cheese and chives to pot; stir gently to coat, breaking potatoes into smaller chunks.

Favorite Green Beans

MAKES 4 SERVINGS

- **1 cup water**
- **1 pound fresh green beans, trimmed**
- **2 tablespoons butter**
- **1 teaspoon garlic salt**
- **⅓ cup grated Parmesan cheese**

1. Pour water into Instant Pot. Place rack in pot; place beans on rack. (Arrange beans perpendicular to rack to prevent beans from falling through. Or use steamer basket.)

2. Secure lid and move pressure release valve to Sealing position. Press Pressure Cook or Manual; cook at high pressure 2 minutes.

3. When cooking is complete, use quick release. Remove rack from pot; drain off and discard cooking liquid. Return beans to pot; add butter and garlic salt. Press Sauté; cook and stir 1 minute or until butter is melted and beans are coated. Stir in cheese.

Sweet and Sour Cabbage

MAKES 4 SERVINGS

- 1½ pounds green or red cabbage or a combination, coarsely chopped
- 2 medium sweet apples (such as Fuji, Honeycrisp or Pink Lady), cut into ½-inch pieces
- ¼ cup water
- 3 tablespoons cider vinegar
- 3 tablespoons packed brown sugar
- 2 tablespoons olive oil
- 1 teaspoon salt
- ½ teaspoon caraway seeds

1. Combine cabbage, apples, water, vinegar, brown sugar, oil, salt and caraway seeds in Instant Pot; mix well.

2. Secure lid and move pressure release valve to Sealing position. Press Pressure Cook or Manual; cook at high pressure 3 minutes.*

3. When cooking is complete, use quick release. If there is excess liquid in pot, press Sauté and cook 3 to 5 minutes or until liquid has evaporated, stirring frequently.

**A cook time of 3 minutes will result in crisp-tender cabbage. For softer cabbage, cook 4 minutes under pressure.*

Simple Squash and Carrots

MAKES 4 TO 6 SERVINGS

- 1½ tablespoons extra virgin olive oil, divided
- 2 medium onions, coarsely chopped
- 2 pounds butternut squash, peeled and cut into 1-inch pieces
- 3 medium carrots, cut diagonally into ½-inch slices
- 1 teaspoon salt, divided
- ¼ teaspoon black pepper
- ½ cup water

1. Press Sauté; heat 1 tablespoon oil in Instant Pot. Add onions; cook and stir 2 minutes or until onions begin to soften. Add squash, carrots, ¾ teaspoon salt and pepper; mix well. Pour in water.

2. Secure lid and move pressure release valve to Sealing position. Press Pressure Cook or Manual; cook at high pressure 1 minute.

3. When cooking is complete, use quick release. Drain excess liquid from pot. Add remaining ½ tablespoon oil and ¼ teaspoon salt; stir gently to coat.

Potato-Cauliflower Mash

MAKES 4 SERVINGS

- **1½ pounds russet potatoes, peeled and cut into 1-inch pieces**
- **1 small cauliflower, cut into florets (4 to 5 cups)**
- **1 cup vegetable broth or water**
- **2 cloves garlic, peeled**
- **1½ teaspoons salt**
- **¼ cup sour cream or plain yogurt**
- **2 tablespoons olive oil**
- **¼ teaspoon black pepper**
- **2 tablespoons chopped fresh chives**

1. Combine potatoes, cauliflower, broth, garlic and salt in Instant Pot; mix well.

2. Secure lid and move pressure release valve to Sealing position. Press Pressure Cook or Manual; cook at high pressure 8 minutes.

3. When cooking is complete, use quick release. Mash vegetables in pot with potato masher until chunky. Add sour cream, oil and pepper; mash until desired consistency is reached. Sprinkle with chives.

Baba Ganoush

MAKES ABOUT 2½ CUPS

- **1½ tablespoons olive oil, divided, plus additional for serving**
- **1½ tablespoons dark sesame oil, divided**
- **2 medium eggplants (about 1 pound each), peeled and cut in half lengthwise**
- **½ cup water**
- **1 clove garlic, minced**
- **¼ cup tahini**
- **2 tablespoons lemon juice**
- **1 teaspoon salt**
- **¼ teaspoon black pepper**
- **Chopped fresh parsley**
- **Pita bread wedges (optional)**

1. Press Sauté; heat half of olive oil and half of sesame oil in Instant Pot. Add two eggplant halves, flat sides down; cook about 5 minutes or until well browned. Remove to plate. Repeat with remaining oil and eggplant halves.

2. Return all eggplant to pot; add water and garlic. Secure lid and move pressure release valve to Sealing position. Press Pressure Cook or Manual; cook at high pressure 8 minutes.

3. When cooking is complete, use quick release. Drain eggplant in colander 5 minutes.

4. Transfer eggplant to medium bowl; mash with potato masher until no large pieces remain.* Add tahini, lemon juice, salt and pepper; stir until well blended. Top with parsley and additional olive oil. Serve with pita wedges, if desired.

**For a smoother dip, transfer cooked eggplant to food processor. Add tahini, lemon juice, salt and pepper; process until smooth.*

Blue Cheese Potatoes

MAKES 4 TO 6 SERVINGS

- **2 pounds red potatoes, peeled and cut into ¾-inch pieces**
- **1¼ cups chopped green onions, divided**
- **1 cup water**
- **2 tablespoons olive oil, divided**
- **1 teaspoon dried basil**
- **1 teaspoon salt**
- **¼ teaspoon black pepper**
- **⅓ cup crumbled blue cheese**

1. Combine potatoes, 1 cup green onions, water, 1 tablespoon oil, basil, 1 teaspoon salt and ¼ teasoon pepper in Instant Pot; mix well.

2. Secure lid and move pressure release valve to Sealing position. Press Pressure Cook or Manual; cook at high pressure 2 minutes.

3. When cooking is complete, use quick release. Drain excess liquid from pot. Gently stir in cheese and remaining 1 tablespoon oil; season with additional salt and pepper. Top with remaining ¼ cup green onions.

Orange-Spiced Glazed Carrots

MAKES 6 SERVINGS

- **1 package (32 ounces) baby carrots**
- **½ cup orange juice**
- **⅓ cup packed brown sugar**
- **3 tablespoons butter, cut into small pieces**
- **¾ teaspoon ground cinnamon**
- **½ teaspoon salt**
- **¼ teaspoon ground nutmeg**
- **¼ cup water**
- **2 tablespoons cornstarch**
- **Grated orange peel (optional)**
- **Chopped fresh parsley (optional)**

1. Combine carrots, orange juice, brown sugar, butter, cinnamon, salt and nutmeg in Instant Pot; mix well.

2. Secure lid and move pressure release valve to Sealing position. Press Pressure Cook or Manual; cook at high pressure 2 minutes.

3. When cooking is complete, use quick release. Stir water into cornstarch in small bowl until smooth. Press Sauté; add cornstarch mixture to pot. Cook and stir 1 to 2 minutes or until sauce thickens. Garnish with orange peel and parsley.

Instant Pot® POULTRY

Greek Braised Cinnamon Chicken

MAKES 4 SERVINGS

- **4 chicken leg quarters (drumstick and thigh, 10 to 12 ounces each)**
- **1¾ teaspoons salt, divided**
- **¾ teaspoon black pepper, divided**
- **¼ plus ⅛ teaspoon ground cinnamon, divided**
- **2 tablespoons olive oil**
- **2 medium onions, chopped**
- **3 cloves garlic, minced**
- **1 can (28 ounces) whole tomatoes, undrained, coarsely chopped or crushed with hands**
- **½ cup chicken broth**
- **1 cinnamon stick**
- **Chopped fresh parsley**
- **Grated Kasseri* or Romano cheese (optional)**

**Kasseri is a semi-hard Greek sheep's milk cheese with a mild buttery and slightly piquant flavor.*

1. Season both sides of chicken with ¾ teaspoon salt, ¼ teaspoon pepper and ⅛ teaspoon ground cinnamon. Press Sauté; heat oil in Instant Pot. Cook chicken in two batches about 5 minutes per side or until browned. Remove to plate. Drain off all but 2 tablespoons fat.

2. Add onions to pot; cook 3 minutes or until softened, scraping up browned bits from bottom of pot. Add garlic and remaining ¼ teaspoon ground cinnamon; cook and stir 1 minute. Stir in tomatoes with liquid, broth, cinnamon stick, remaining 1 teaspoon salt and ½ teaspoon pepper; mix well. Return chicken to pot, skin side up, pressing down to partially submerge chicken in sauce.

3. Secure lid and move pressure release valve to Sealing position. Press Pressure Cook or Manual; cook at high pressure 11 minutes.

4. When cooking is complete, use natural release for 5 minutes, then release remaining pressure. Remove chicken to serving platter; tent with foil.

5. Press Sauté; cook 5 to 10 minutes or until sauce is slightly reduced and thickened. Pour sauce over chicken; sprinkle with parsley and serve with cheese, if desired.

Chicken Tinga

MAKES 6 SERVINGS

- **1 tablespoon vegetable oil**
- **1 medium white onion, quartered**
- **3 medium tomatillos, husks removed and cut in half**
- **3 cloves garlic**
- **1 teaspoon dried oregano**
- **½ teaspoon ground cumin**
- **1 can (about 14 ounces) diced fire-roasted tomatoes**
- **2 canned chipotle peppers in adobo sauce**
- **2 tablespoons cider vinegar**
- **1¼ teaspoons salt**
- **2 pounds boneless skinless chicken thighs**
- **2 bay leaves**
- **Corn tortillas, heated**
- **Optional toppings: thinly sliced onion, shredded cabbage, chopped fresh cilantro and/or lime wedges**

1. Press Sauté; heat oil in Instant Pot. Add onion, tomatillos and garlic, cut sides down; cook without stirring about 5 minutes or until vegetables are browned in spots. Stir vegetables; cook 3 minutes for additional browning. Add oregano and cumin; cook and stir 1 minute. Add tomatoes; cook and stir 2 minutes. Stir in chipotle peppers, vinegar and salt; mix well.

2. Use hand-held immersion blender to purée mixure in pot until smooth (you will need to tilt pot for blending). Or transfer mixture to blender or food processor; blend until smooth and return to pot.

3. Add chicken and bay leaves to pot, submerging chicken in sauce. Secure lid and move pressure release valve to Sealing position. Press Pressure Cook or Manual; cook at high pressure 8 minutes.

4. When cooking is complete, use natural release for 5 minutes, then release remaining pressure. Remove chicken to medium bowl; set aside 10 minutes or until cool enough to handle. Meanwhile, press Sauté; cook about 5 minutes or until sauce reduces slightly. Remove and discard bay leaves.

5. Shred chicken into bite-size pieces. Add about half of sauce from pot; toss to coat. Serve chicken with tortillas, desired toppings and remaining sauce.

Chicken Vindaloo

MAKES 4 SERVINGS

- **1 onion, coarsely chopped**
- **1/3 cup white vinegar**
- **2 tablespoons tomato paste**
- **1 tablespoon minced fresh ginger**
- **3 cloves garlic**
- **1½ teaspoons paprika**
- **1 teaspoon salt**
- **1 teaspoon ground coriander**
- **1 teaspoon ground turmeric**
- **½ teaspoon dry mustard**
- **½ teaspoon ground red pepper**
- **½ teaspoon ground cumin**
- **1½ pounds boneless skinless chicken thighs**
- **¼ cup water**
- **Hot cooked rice (optional)**
- **Chopped fresh cilantro**

1. Combine onion, vinegar, tomato paste, ginger, garlic, paprika, salt, coriander, turmeric, mustard, red pepper and cumin in food processor or blender; process until smooth.

2. Place chicken in large resealable food storage bag. Pour spice mixture over chicken; seal bag and massage mixture into chicken, making sure all pieces are completely coated. Marinate in refrigerator at least 1 hour or overnight.

3. Pour chicken and marinade into Instant Pot; stir in water. Secure lid and move pressure release valve to Sealing position. Press Pressure Cook or Manual; cook at high pressure 7 minutes.

4. When cooking is complete, use natural release for 5 minutes, then release remaining pressure. Remove chicken to plate; tent with foil to keep warm.

5. Press Sauté; cook about 5 minutes or until sauce reduces and thickens slightly, stirring frequently. Pour sauce over chicken; serve with rice, if desired. Sprinkle with cilantro.

Three Bean Turkey Chili

MAKES 8 SERVINGS

- 1 tablespoon olive oil
- 1 pound ground turkey
- 1 medium onion, chopped
- 2 tablespoons chili powder
- 1½ teaspoons smoked paprika
- 1½ teaspoons ground cumin
- 1 can (about 28 ounces) diced tomatoes
- 1 can (about 15 ounces) chickpeas, rinsed and drained
- 1 can (about 15 ounces) kidney beans, rinsed and drained
- 1 can (about 15 ounces) black beans, rinsed and drained
- 1 can (6 ounces) tomato sauce
- 1 can (4 ounces) chopped green chiles
- ⅓ cup chicken broth or water
- 1½ teaspoons salt

1. Press Sauté; heat oil in Instant Pot. Add turkey and onion; cook and stir about 6 minutes or until turkey is no longer pink. Add chili powder, paprika and cumin; cook and stir 2 minutes. Stir in tomatoes, chickpeas, beans, tomato sauce, chiles, broth and salt; mix well.

2. Secure lid and move pressure release valve to Sealing position. Press Pressure Cook or Manual; cook at high pressure 15 minutes.

3. When cooking is complete, use natural release for 10 minutes, then release remaining pressure. If there is excess liquid in pot, press Sauté and cook 5 minutes or until chili is thickened.

Quick Moroccan Chicken

MAKES 6 SERVINGS

- ¼ cup dry white wine
- ¼ cup chicken broth
- 2 tablespoons olive oil
- 2 cloves garlic, minced
- 2 teaspoons dried oregano
- 1 teaspoon paprika
- ½ teaspoon salt
- ½ teaspoon black pepper
- 6 bone-in chicken thighs, (2½ to 3 pounds), skin removed
- 1 lemon, cut into ¼-inch slices
- ¾ cup pitted prunes
- ½ cup pitted green olives
- ¼ cup currants or raisins
- 2 tablespoons capers
- Hot cooked rice or couscous
- Chopped fresh parsley or cilantro (optional)

1. Combine wine, broth, oil, garlic, oregano, paprika, salt and pepper in Instant Pot; mix well. Add chicken; turn to coat. Tuck lemon slices between chicken thighs. Top with prunes, olives, currants and capers. (Do not stir.)

2. Secure lid and move pressure release valve to Sealing position. Press Pressure Cook or Manual; cook at high pressure 12 minutes.

3. When cooking is complete, use natural release for 10 minutes, then release remaining pressure. Serve chicken with rice; sprinkle with parsley, if desired.

Easy Chinese Chicken

MAKES 4 SERVINGS

- 1 cut-up whole chicken (3 to 4 pounds)
- 1/4 cup dry sherry
- 1/4 cup reduced-sodium soy sauce
- 4 cloves garlic, minced
- 1 tablespoon minced fresh ginger
- 1/4 teaspoon red pepper flakes

1. Place chicken in large resealable food storage bag. Combine sherry, soy sauce, garlic, ginger and red pepper flakes in small bowl; mix well. Pour over chicken; seal bag and turn to coat. Marinate chicken in refrigerator at least 30 minutes or up to 4 hours, turning once or twice.

2. Place chicken and marinade in Instant Pot. Secure lid and move pressure release valve to Sealing position. Press Pressure Cook or Manual; cook at high pressure 13 minutes. Preheat broiler. Line large baking sheet with foil.

3. When cooking is complete, use natural release for 10 minutes, then release remaining pressure. Place chicken on prepared baking sheet, skin side up.

4. Broil 5 to 7 minutes or until skin is browned and crisp, basting once with cooking liquid from pot.

Pesto Turkey Meatballs

MAKES 4 SERVINGS

- 1 pound ground turkey
- ⅓ cup pesto sauce
- ⅓ cup grated Parmesan cheese, plus additional for garnish
- ¼ cup panko bread crumbs
- 1 egg
- 2 green onions, finely chopped
- ½ teaspoon salt, divided
- 2 tablespoons olive oil
- 2 cloves garlic, minced
- ⅛ teaspoon red pepper flakes
- 1 can (28 ounces) whole tomatoes, undrained, crushed with hands or coarsely chopped
- 1 tablespoon tomato paste
- Hot cooked pasta (optional)
- Chopped fresh basil (optional)

1. Combine turkey, pesto, ⅓ cup cheese, panko, egg, green onions and ¼ teaspoon salt in medium bowl; mix well. Shape mixture into 24 (1¼-inch) meatballs. Refrigerate meatballs while preparing sauce.

2. Press Sauté; heat oil in Instant Pot. Add garlic and red pepper flakes; cook and stir 1 minute. Add tomatoes with liquid, tomato paste and remaining ¼ teaspoon salt; cook 3 minutes or until sauce begins to simmer, stirring occasionally.

3. Remove about 1 cup sauce from pot. Arrange meatballs in single layer in pot; pour reserved sauce over meatballs.

4. Secure lid and move pressure release valve to Sealing position. Press Pressure Cook or Manual; cook at high pressure 10 minutes.

5. When cooking is complete, use natural release for 10 minutes, then release remaining pressure. If sauce is too thin, press Sauté and cook 5 minutes or until sauce thickens, stirring frequently. Serve meatballs over pasta, if desired. Garnish with additional cheese and basil.

Rotisserie-Style Chicken

MAKES 4 SERVINGS

- 1 whole chicken (about 4 pounds)
- 2 tablespoons rotisserie chicken seasoning (see Tip)
- 1 tablespoon butter
- 1 tablespoon olive oil
- 1 cup chicken broth
- Fresh parsley sprigs and lemon wedges (optional)

1. Pat chicken dry. Tie drumsticks together with kitchen string and tuck wing tips under. Sprinkle seasoning inside cavity and over all sides of chicken, pressing to adhere.

2. Press Sauté; heat butter and oil in Instant Pot. Add chicken, breast side up; cook about 5 minutes or until browned. Turn chicken over using tongs and spatula; cook about 5 minutes or until browned. Remove chicken to plate.

3. Add broth to pot; cook 1 minute, scraping up browned bits from bottom of pot. Place rack in pot; place chicken on rack, breast side up.

4. Secure lid and move pressure release valve to Sealing position. Press Pressure Cook or Manual; cook at high pressure 21 minutes.

5. When cooking is complete, use natural release for 15 minutes, then release remaining pressure. Remove chicken to cutting board; tent with foil and let stand 10 minutes before carving. If desired, strain cooking liquid and serve with chicken. Garnish with parsley and lemon wedges.

TIP

Rotisserie chicken seasoning is available in the spice section of many supermarkets. If unavailable, you can use a basic poultry seasoning or Italian seasoning combined with 1 teaspoon salt and 1 teaspoon paprika. Or use your favorite seasoning blend.

Note

When fully cooked, the temperature of the chicken (tested in the thigh) should be 165°F. A chicken larger than 4 pounds may take an additional 3 minutes to cook, while a smaller chicken will take a few minutes less.

Butter Chicken

MAKES 4 TO 6 SERVINGS

- 2 tablespoons butter
- 1 onion, chopped
- 4 cloves garlic, minced
- 1 teaspoon minced fresh ginger
- 1 teaspoon ground turmeric
- 1 teaspoon ground coriander
- 1 teaspoon garam masala
- 1 teaspoon ground cumin
- ½ teaspoon ground red pepper
- ½ teaspoon paprika
- 1 can (about 14 ounces) diced tomatoes
- ¾ teaspoon salt
- 2 pounds boneless skinless chicken breasts, cut into 2-inch pieces
- ½ cup whipping cream
- Chopped fresh cilantro
- Hot cooked rice (optional)

1. Press Sauté; melt butter in Instant Pot. Add onion; cook and stir about 4 minutes or until onion begins to turn golden. Add garlic and ginger; cook and stir 1 minute. Add turmeric, coriander, garam masala, cumin, red pepper and paprika; cook and stir 30 seconds. Add tomatoes and salt; cook and stir 2 minutes. Stir in chicken; mix well.

2. Secure lid and move pressure release valve to Sealing position. Press Pressure Cook or Manual; cook at high pressure 8 minutes.

3. When cooking is complete, use natural release for 10 minutes, then release remaining pressure.

4. Press Sauté; adjust heat to low. Stir in cream; cook 5 minutes or until heated through. Sprinkle with cilantro; serve with rice, if desired.

Instant Pot BEEF

Brisket Tacos

MAKES ABOUT 6 SERVINGS

- 1 beef brisket (2½ to 3 pounds)
- 2 teaspoons salt
- 2 teaspoons chili powder
- 2 teaspoons smoked paprika
- 1 teaspoon ground cumin
- ½ teaspoon black pepper
- 3 tablespoons vegetable oil, divided
- 2 medium onions, cut in half and cut into ¼-inch slices, divided
- ¾ cup beef broth, divided
- 3 cloves garlic, minced
- 2 medium poblano peppers, cut into ¼-inch slices
- Corn tortillas, heated
- Optional toppings: chunky salsa, fresh cilantro leaves, queso fresco, shredded cabbage and/or sliced avocado

1. Trim fat on brisket to ¼ inch. Pat brisket dry; cut in half crosswise. Combine salt, chili powder, smoked paprika, cumin and black pepper in small bowl; mix well. Rub spice mixture over all sides of brisket to coat completely. Let stand at room temperature 30 minutes or cover and refrigerate overnight.

2. Press Sauté; heat 1 tablespoon oil in Instant Pot. Add half of brisket, fat side down; cook 4 to 5 minutes per side or until browned. Remove to plate. Repeat with 1 tablespoon oil and remaining half of brisket. Add 1 onion and 2 tablespoons broth to pot; cook 3 minutes or until softened, scraping up browned bits from bottom of pot. Add garlic; cook and stir 1 minute. Stir in remaining broth; mix well. Return brisket to pot, fat side up. (Crowd brisket pieces next to each other, not stacked on top.)

3. Secure lid and move pressure release valve to Sealing position. Press Pressure Cook or Manual; cook at high pressure 1 hour 15 minutes.

4. When cooking is complete, use natural release. Remove brisket to large plate; let stand 10 minutes. Meanwhile, preheat broiler. Line baking sheet with foil.

5. Combine remaining onion and poblano peppers on prepared baking sheet. Drizzle with remaining 1 tablespoon oil and 2 tablespoons cooking liquid from pot; toss to coat. Spread vegetables on baking sheet. Broil 6 to 8 minutes or until vegetables begin to brown, stirring occasionally. Remove to medium bowl.

6. Shred brisket into bite-size pieces; transfer to same baking sheet. Drizzle with ⅓ cup cooking liquid from pot; toss to coat. Spread out meat on baking sheet. Broil about 5 minutes or until edges begin to char. Toss with additional cooking liquid, if desired. Serve brisket and vegetables in tortillas with desired toppings.

Southwestern Sloppy Joes

MAKES 6 SERVINGS

- 1 pound ground beef
- 1 medium onion, chopped
- 1 stalk celery, chopped
- 1 can (10 ounces) diced tomatoes with green chiles
- 1 can (8 ounces) tomato sauce
- 1 tablespoon packed brown sugar
- 1 teaspoon chili powder
- 1 teaspoon ground cumin
- ¾ teaspoon salt
- ½ teaspoon garlic powder
- 6 hamburger buns, split

1. Press Sauté; add beef, onion and celery to Instant Pot. Cook 6 to 8 minutes or until beef is no longer pink, stirring to break up meat. Drain fat and any excess liquid. Stir in tomatoes, tomato sauce, brown sugar, chili powder, cumin, salt and garlic powder; mix well.

2. Secure lid and move pressure release valve to Sealing position. Press Pressure Cook or Manual; cook at high pressure 10 minutes.

3. When cooking is complete, use natural release for 10 minutes, then release remaining pressure. Press Sauté; cook 5 minutes or until mixture thickens slightly, stirring occasionally. Serve on buns.

Perfect Pot Roast

MAKES 6 SERVINGS

- 1 boneless beef chuck roast (3 to 4 pounds)
- 2 tablespoons steak seasoning,* divided
- 1 tablespoon olive oil
- 1 can (about 14 ounces) diced tomatoes
- ½ cup beef broth
- 2 tablespoons prepared horseradish
- ½ teaspoon salt
- 6 carrots, cut into 2-inch pieces
- 2 onions, quartered
- 2 stalks celery, cut into 1-inch slices
- 2 pounds Yukon gold potatoes, cut into 1-inch pieces
- 2 tablespoons water
- 2 tablespoons cornstarch

*Steak seasoning can be found in the spice section of many supermarkets; it is typically a blend of salt, black pepper, garlic powder, onion powder, paprika and additional spices.

1. Season beef with 1 tablespoon steak seasoning. Press Sauté; heat oil in Instant Pot. Add beef; cook about 5 minutes per side or until well browned. Remove to plate.

2. Add tomatoes and broth; cook 2 minutes, scraping up browned bits from bottom of pot. Stir in horseradish, salt and remaining 1 tablespoon steak seasoning. Add carrots, onions and celery; mix well. Return beef to pot.

3. Secure lid and move pressure release valve to Sealing position. Press Pressure Cook or Manual; cook at high pressure 45 minutes.

4. When cooking is complete, use natural release for 10 minutes, then release remaining pressure. Remove beef to clean plate; add potatoes to pot. Secure lid and move pressure release valve to Sealing position. Press Pressure Cook or Manual; cook at high pressure 2 minutes.

5. When cooking is complete, use quick release. Remove potatoes to bowl with slotted spoon. Stir water into cornstarch in small bowl until smooth. Press Sauté; add cornstarch mixture to pot. Cook and stir 2 minutes or until sauce thickens. Slice beef; serve with vegetables and sauce.

Classic Beef Stew

MAKES 8 SERVINGS

- 1 boneless beef chuck roast (about 3 pounds), trimmed
- 2 teaspoons salt
- ½ teaspoon black pepper
- 2 tablespoons olive oil
- 3 large onions, halved and cut into ¼-inch slices
- 6 medium carrots, cut into 1½-inch pieces
- 1 package (8 ounces) mushrooms, thickly sliced
- 4 cloves garlic, minced
- 1 teaspoon herbes de Provence or dried thyme
- 1 teaspoon smoked paprika
- ½ cup beef broth
- 2 tablespoons soy sauce
- 2 tablespoons water
- 2 tablespoons cornstarch
- 3 tablespoons chopped fresh parsley
- Hot cooked egg noodles or mashed potatoes (optional)

1. Season beef with 2 teaspoons salt and ½ teaspoon pepper. Press Sauté; heat oil in Instant Pot. Add beef; cook about 5 minutes per side or until well browned. Remove to cutting board; cut into 1½-inch pieces, trimming off and discarding excess fat.

2. Add onions to pot; cook 5 minutes, scraping up browned bits from bottom of pot. Add carrots, mushrooms, garlic, herbes de Provence and smoked paprika; cook and stir 4 minutes or until vegetables begin to soften. Add broth, soy sauce and beef; mix well.

3. Secure lid and move pressure release valve to Sealing position. Press Pressure Cook or Manual; cook at high pressure 25 minutes.

4. When cooking is complete, use natural release for 15 minutes, then release remaining pressure. Skim fat from surface. Stir water into cornstarch in small bowl until smooth. Press Sauté; add cornstarch mixture to pot. Cook and stir 2 minutes or until stew thickens. Stir in parsley; season with additional salt and pepper. Serve over noodles, if desired.

Italian Short Ribs

MAKES 4 TO 6 SERVINGS

- **3 pounds beef short ribs, trimmed**
- **1½ teaspoons salt**
- **1 teaspoon black pepper**
- **1½ tablespoons vegetable oil**
- **2 large onions, cut into ¼-inch slices**
- **2 packages (8 ounces each) baby bella or cremini mushrooms, quartered**
- **2 cloves garlic, minced**
- **1 teaspoon Italian seasoning**
- **⅓ cup dry red wine**
- **⅓ cup beef broth**
- **1 tablespoon balsamic vinegar**

1. Season short ribs with salt and pepper. Press Sauté; heat oil in Instant Pot. Add short ribs in two batches; cook about 10 minutes or until browned on all sides. Remove to plate.

2. Add onions and mushrooms to pot; cook about 5 minutes or until mushrooms begin to release their liquid, stirring occasionally and scraping up browned bits from bottom of pot. Add garlic and Italian seasoning; cook and stir 1 minute. Add wine; cook about 3 minutes or until reduced by half. Stir in broth. Return short ribs to pot.

3. Secure lid and move pressure release valve to Sealing position. Press Pressure Cook or Manual; cook at high pressure 30 minutes.

4. When cooking is complete, use natural release for 10 minutes, then release remaining pressure. Remove short ribs and mushrooms to serving plate; tent with foil. Let cooking liquid stand 10 minutes;* skim fat from surface. Stir in vinegar. Serve sauce over short ribs and mushrooms.

**Skimming fat is easiest when the sauce is refrigerated several hours or overnight. Reheat sauce and short ribs before serving.*

Simple Salsa Brisket

MAKES 4 SERVINGS

- **1 beef brisket (2½ to 3 pounds)**
- **1¼ teaspoons salt, divided**
- **½ teaspoon black pepper**
- **2 tablespoons vegetable oil, divided**
- **2 medium onions, chopped**
- **1 cup chunky salsa**
- **2 teaspoons cornstarch**

1. Trim fat on brisket to ¼ inch. Cut brisket in half crosswise; season with 1 teaspoon salt and pepper. Press Sauté; heat 1 tablespoon oil in Instant Pot. Add half of brisket; cook 4 to 5 minutes per side or until browned. Remove to plate. Repeat with remaining 1 tablespoon oil and half of brisket.

2. Add onions and remaining ¼ teaspoon salt to pot; cook and stir about 4 minutes or until softened, scraping up browned bits from bottom of pot. Stir in salsa; mix well. Return brisket to pot, fat side up; press into salsa mixture. (Crowd brisket pieces next to each other, not stacked on top.)

3. Secure lid and move pressure release valve to Sealing position. Press Pressure Cook or Manual; cook at high pressure 60 minutes.

4. When cooking is complete, use natural release for 15 minutes, then release remaining pressure. Remove brisket to cutting board or clean plate; tent with foil and let rest 10 minutes.

5. Meanwhile, press Sauté; cook sauce in pot 10 minutes or until reduced by one third. Place cornstarch in small bowl; stir in ¼ cup sauce from pot until smooth. Add cornstarch mixture to pot; cook and stir 2 minutes or until sauce thickens. Slice brisket against the grain; serve with sauce.

Barbecue Beef Sandwiches

MAKES 4 SERVINGS

- 1 boneless beef chuck roast (about 2½ pounds), cut in half
- 2 tablespoons Southwest seasoning
- 1 tablespoon vegetable oil
- ½ cup beef broth
- 1½ cups barbecue sauce, divided
- 4 sandwich or pretzel buns, split
- 1⅓ cups prepared coleslaw* (preferably vinegar based)

**Vinegar-based coleslaws provide a perfect complement to the rich beef; they can often be found at the salad bar, deli counter or prepared foods section of large supermarkets.*

1. Sprinkle both sides of beef with Southwest seasoning. Press Sauté; heat oil in Instant Pot. Add beef; cook about 6 minutes per side or until browned. Remove to plate.

2. Add broth to pot; cook 2 minutes, scraping up browned bits from bottom of pot. Stir in ½ cup barbecue sauce. Return beef to pot; turn to coat.

3. Secure lid and move pressure release valve to Sealing position. Press Pressure Cook or Manual; cook at high pressure 60 minutes.

4. When cooking is complete, use natural release for 15 minutes, then release remaining pressure. Remove beef to large bowl; let stand until cool enough to handle. Shred beef into bite-size pieces. Stir in remaining 1 cup barbecue sauce.

5. Fill buns with beef mixture; top with coleslaw.

Taco-Seasoned Pot Roast

MAKES 4 TO 6 SERVINGS

- **1 boneless beef chuck roast (2½ to 3 pounds)**
- **1 package (about 1 ounce) taco seasoning mix, divided**
- **1½ tablespoons vegetable oil**
- **3 medium onions**
- **¾ cup water, divided**
- **¾ cup chunky salsa, divided**
- **½ teaspoon salt**
- **1½ pounds small unpeeled red potatoes (1 to 1½ inches)***
- **5 medium carrots, cut into 2-inch pieces**

If small potatoes are not available, use medium red potatoes and cut into 1-inch pieces.

1. Season beef on all sides with 4 teaspoons taco seasoning. Press Sauté; heat oil in Instant Pot. Add beef; cook 6 to 8 minutes per side or until very well browned. Meanwhile, chop 1 onion. Cut remaining 2 onions into six wedges each.

2. Remove beef to plate. Add chopped onion and ¼ cup water to pot; cook 2 minutes, scraping up browned bits from bottom of pot. Stir in ½ cup salsa, remaining ½ cup water, taco seasoning and salt; mix well. Return beef to pot; turn to coat.

3. Secure lid and move pressure release valve to Sealing position. Press Pressure Cook or Manual; cook at high pressure 60 minutes.

4. When cooking is complete, use natural release. Remove beef to clean plate; tent with foil to keep warm. Add potatoes, carrots and onion wedges to pot; stir gently to submerge vegetables in cooking liquid. Secure lid and move pressure release valve to Sealing position. Press Pressure Cook or Manual; cook at high pressure 4 minutes.

5. When cooking is complete, use quick release. Remove vegetables to serving platter or large bowl with slotted spoon. Skim fat from surface of sauce. Press Sauté; add remaining ¼ cup salsa to pot and cook about 5 minutes or until sauce is slightly reduced and thickened. Serve sauce with beef and vegetables.

Italian Beef Ragu

MAKES 6 SERVINGS

- 1 boneless beef chuck roast (about 2 pounds), cut into 2-inch pieces
- ½ teaspoon salt
- ½ teaspoon black pepper
- 1 tablespoon olive oil
- 1 onion, chopped
- ½ cup plus 2 tablespoons beef broth, divided
- 1 jar (24 ounces) garlic and herb pasta sauce
- ¼ cup plus 1 tablespoon red wine vinegar, divided
- Hot cooked pappardelle pasta
- Slivered fresh basil (optional)
- Grated Parmesan cheese (optional)

1. Season beef with ½ teaspoon salt and ½ teaspoon pepper. Press Sauté; heat oil in Instant Pot. Add beef in two batches; cook about 5 minutes or until browned. Remove to plate. Add onion and 2 tablespoons broth to pot; cook 3 minutes or until softened, scraping up browned bits from bottom of pot. Reserve ¾ cup pasta sauce; set aside. Add remaining pasta sauce, ½ cup broth and ¼ cup vinegar to pot; mix well. Return beef to pot; stir to coat.

2. Secure lid and move pressure release valve to Sealing position. Press Pressure Cook or Manual; cook at high pressure 45 minutes.

3. When cooking is complete, use natural release for 15 minutes, then release remaining pressure. Remove beef to large bowl; let stand 5 minutes or until cool enough to handle.

4. Meanwhile, press Sauté; adjust heat to low. Add reserved ¾ cup pasta sauce and remaining 1 tablespoon vinegar to pot; cook 5 minutes, stirring occasionally.

5. Shred beef into bite-size pieces; stir into sauce. Taste and season with additional salt and pepper. Serve over pasta; garnish with basil and cheese.

Instant Pot PORK

Tacos al Pastor

MAKES 6 TO 8 SERVINGS

- 1 medium pineapple
- 1 small red onion, coarsely chopped
- Juice of 1 orange
- Juice of 1 lime
- 2 canned chipotle peppers in adobo sauce
- 1 tablespoon white vinegar
- 1 tablespoon chili powder
- 2 teaspoons salt
- 2 cloves garlic
- 1 teaspoon ground cumin
- ½ teaspoon black pepper
- 2½ pounds boneless pork shoulder, cut into 2-inch pieces
- Flour or corn tortillas, heated
- Optional toppings: pickled red onion, fresh cilantro leaves, diced avocado and/or lime wedges

1. Peel and core pineapple; set aside half for topping. Coarsely chop remaining half; place in food processor with onion, orange juice, lime juice, chipotle peppers, vinegar, chili powder, salt, garlic, cumin and black pepper. Process until smooth.

2. Place pork in large resealable food storage bag; pour marinade over pork. Seal bag and turn to coat. Marinate in refrigerator at least 4 hours or overnight.

3. Pour pork and marinade into Instant Pot. Secure lid and move pressure release valve to Sealing position. Press Pressure Cook or Manual; cook at high pressure 40 minutes.

4. Meanwhile, cut reserved pineapple half into ½-inch pieces. Preheat broiler. Line baking sheet with foil. Spread pineapple on one third of baking sheet.

5. When cooking is complete, use natural release for 10 minutes, then release remaining pressure. Remove pork to prepared baking sheet; break into smaller chunks and spread out next to pineapple. Broil 5 to 8 minutes or until pork and pineapple begin to brown and char in spots.

6. Meanwhile, press Sauté; cook liquid in pot 5 to 10 minutes or until reduced and thickened slightly. Drizzle sauce over pork; serve pork and pineapple in tortillas with desired toppings.

Spicy Pork Po' Boys

MAKES 4 SERVINGS

- **4 teaspoons chili powder**
- **2 teaspoons salt**
- **2 teaspoons onion powder**
- **2 teaspoons garlic powder**
- **2 teaspoons paprika**
- **1½ teaspoons black pepper**
- **½ teaspoon ground red pepper**
- **1 pound boneless pork ribs**
- **½ cup pineapple juice**
- **1 tablespoon hot pepper sauce**
- **1 tablespoon balsamic vinegar**
- **1 teaspoon Worcestershire sauce**
- **½ cup ketchup**
- **4 French rolls, toasted**
- **½ cup prepared coleslaw**

1. Combine chili powder, salt, onion powder, garlic powder, paprika, black pepper and red pepper in small bowl; mix well. Rub mixture over pork, coating all sides. Cover and refrigerate at least 3 hours or overnight.

2. Place ribs in Instant Pot. Combine pineapple juice, hot pepper sauce, vinegar and Worcestershire sauce in small bowl; pour over ribs.

3. Secure lid and move pressure release valve to Sealing position. Press Pressure Cook or Manual; cook at high pressure 25 minutes.

4. When cooking is complete, use natural release for 10 minutes, then release remaining pressure. Remove ribs to large bowl. Press Sauté; add ketchup to pot. Cook 2 to 3 minutes or until sauce thickens, stirring frequently.

5. Shred pork into bite-size pieces. Add ½ cup sauce; toss to coat. Add additional sauce as needed or serve remaining sauce on the side. Serve pork on rolls with coleslaw.

Meaty Sausage Spaghetti

MAKES 6 TO 8 SERVINGS

- 1 tablespoon olive oil
- 1 medium onion, chopped
- 2 cloves garlic, minced
- 1 package (20 ounces) bulk Italian sausage
- 1 cup chopped yellow, red and/or green bell peppers
- 1 can (about 14 ounces) crushed tomatoes
- 1 can (about 14 ounces) diced tomatoes
- 2½ teaspoons salt
- 2 teaspoons dried basil
- 1 teaspoon dried oregano
- ¼ teaspoon black pepper
- 1 package (16 ounces) uncooked spaghetti, broken in half
- 2½ to 3½ cups water, divided
- Grated Parmesan cheese

1. Press Sauté; heat oil in Instant Pot. Add onion and garlic; cook and stir 3 minutes or until onion is softened. Add sausage; cook until browned, stirring to break up meat. Drain fat. Add bell peppers; cook and stir 2 minutes. Add crushed tomatoes, diced tomatoes, salt, basil, oregano and black pepper; mix well.

2. Add pasta to pot; stir gently to allow some liquid to get between strands of spaghetti to prevent sticking. Add 2½ cups water.

3. Secure lid and move pressure release valve to Sealing position. Press Pressure Cook or Manual; cook at high pressure 5 minutes.

4. When cooking is complete, use quick release. Press Sauté; add ½ cup water. Cook and stir 2 minutes or until pasta is al dente, adding remaining ½ cup water if necessary to reach desired consistency. Season with additional salt and black pepper. Serve immediately with cheese.

Shredded Pork Wraps

MAKES 6 SERVINGS

- **1¼ cups salsa, divided**
- **¼ cup water**
- **1 boneless pork loin roast (about 2 pounds), cut in half crosswise**
- **1 tablespoon cornstarch**
- **6 (8-inch) flour tortillas**
- **3 cups broccoli slaw mix**
- **¾ cup (3 ounces) shredded Cheddar cheese**

1. Combine 1 cup salsa and water in Instant Pot; mix well. Add pork; turn to coat.

2. Secure lid and move pressure release valve to Sealing position. Press Pressure Cook or Manual; cook at high pressure 30 minutes.

3. When cooking is complete, use natural release for 10 minutes, then release remaining pressure. Remove pork to plate; let stand until cool enough to handle. Shred or cut pork into bite-size pieces.

4. Stir 2 tablespoons cooking liquid from pot into cornstarch in small bowl until smooth. Press Sauté; add cornstarch mixture and remaining ¼ cup salsa to pot. Cook and stir about 2 minutes or until sauce thickens. Turn off heat. Remove 1 cup sauce from pot; reserve for dipping. Add pork to pot; stir to coat.

5. Top tortillas with pork mixture, broccoli slaw and cheese. Fold bottom edge of each tortilla over filling; fold in sides. Roll up completely to enclose filling. Serve wraps with reserved sauce.

Spicy Pork and Vegetable Stew

MAKES 6 SERVINGS

- **2 tablespoons olive oil, divided**
- **1½ pounds boneless pork loin, cut into 1-inch pieces**
- **1 package (8 ounces) mushrooms, thickly sliced (1 inch)**
- **1 medium onion, chopped**
- **½ teaspoon dried thyme**
- **½ teaspoon black pepper**
- **¼ to ½ teaspoon red pepper flakes**
- **¼ teaspoon dried oregano**
- **1 can (about 14 ounces) diced tomatoes**
- **1½ teaspoons salt**
- **1 small butternut squash, peeled and cut into ¾-inch pieces (about 3 cups)**
- **2 red bell peppers, cut into 1-inch pieces**
- **Fresh oregano (optional)**

1. Press Sauté; heat 1 tablespoon oil in Instant Pot Add half of pork; cook 5 minutes or until browned, stirring occasionally. Remove to plate. Repeat with remaining 1 tablespoon oil and remaining pork.

2. Add mushrooms; cook about 3 minutes or until mushrooms begin to release their liquid, stirring occasionally and scraping up browned bits from bottom of pot. Add onion, thyme, black pepper, red pepper flakes and dried oregano; cook and stir 1 minute. Stir in tomatoes, salt and pork; mix well.

3. Secure lid and move pressure release valve to Sealing position. Press Pressure Cook or Manual; cook at high pressure 5 minutes.

4. When cooking is complete, use natural release for 5 minutes, then release remaining pressure. Add squash and bell peppers to pot. Secure lid and move pressure release valve to Sealing position. Press Pressure Cook or Manual; cook at high pressure 3 minutes.

5. When cooking is complete, use quick release. Garnish with fresh oregano.

Perfect BBQ Ribs

MAKES 4 SERVINGS

- 1 rack pork baby back ribs (about 3 pounds)
- ⅓ cup barbecue seasoning or grilling rub
- 2 cups apple juice
- ¼ cup cider vinegar
- 1 tablespoon liquid smoke
- 1 cup barbecue sauce, plus additional for serving

1. Remove membrane covering bones on underside of ribs. Rub barbecue seasoning generously over both sides of ribs, pressing to adhere.

2. Combine apple juice, vinegar and liquid smoke in Instant Pot; mix well. Stand ribs vertically in liquid, coiling ribs into a ring to fit in pot.

3. Secure lid and move pressure release valve to Sealing position. Press Pressure Cook or Manual; cook at high pressure 20 minutes. Preheat broiler. Line baking sheet with foil.

4. When cooking is complete, use natural release for 5 minutes, then release remaining pressure. Remove ribs to prepared baking sheet, meaty side up. Brush both sides of ribs with 1 cup barbecue sauce.

5. Broil about 5 minutes or until sauce begins to bubble and char. Cut into individual ribs; serve with additional sauce.

Pork Carnitas

MAKES 6 SERVINGS

- 2 tablespoons chili powder
- 1 tablespoon salt
- 1 tablespoon dried oregano
- 1 teaspoon ground cumin
- 1 medium onion, quartered
- 2 pounds pork leg, shoulder or roast, trimmed, cut into 4 pieces
- 2 bay leaves
- 1½ cups water
- Hot cooked rice
- Optional toppings: black beans, halved cherry tomatoes, sliced avocado, crumbled cotija cheese, lime wedges and/or fresh cilantro leaves

1. Combine chili powder, salt, oregano and cumin in small bowl; mix well. Place onion in Instant Pot; place pork on top of onion. Sprinkle all over with spice mixture. Add bay leaves. Pour water into pot.

2. Secure lid and move pressure release valve to Sealing position. Press Pressure Cook or Manual; cook at high pressure 1 hour 15 minutes.

3. When cooking is complete, use natural release for 10 minutes, then release remaining pressure. Remove pork from liquid with tongs; place in 13×9-inch baking pan or on baking sheet lined with foil. Preheat broiler.

4. Remove and discard bay leaves from cooking liquid. Press Sauté; cook 10 minutes to reduce slightly. Meanwhile, separate pork into large shreds with tongs; spread out in baking pan. Broil about 3 minutes or until browned.

5. Pull pork into smaller shreds with tongs or two forks. Place pork in medium bowl; add 1 cup cooking liquid and toss to coat. Add additional liquid, if desired. Serve pork over rice with desired toppings.

Pork Roast with Fruit

MAKES 6 TO 8 SERVINGS

- **2 cups water**
- **2 tablespoons salt**
- **1 tablespoon sugar**
- **1 teaspoon dried thyme**
- **1 bay leaf**
- **½ teaspoon black pepper**
- **1 boneless pork loin roast (3 to 3½ pounds)**
- **1 tablespoon olive oil**
- **⅓ cup dry red wine**
- **Juice of ½ lemon**
- **2 cloves garlic, minced**
- **2 cups green grapes**
- **1 cup dried apricots**
- **1 cup dried prunes**

1. Combine water, salt, sugar, thyme, bay leaf and pepper in medium bowl; mix well. Place pork in large resealable food storage bag. Pour brine over pork; seal bag and turn to coat. Refrigerate overnight or up to 2 days, turning occasionally.

2. Remove pork from brine; discard liquid. Pat dry with paper towels. Press Sauté; heat oil in Instant Pot. Add pork; cook about 10 minutes or until browned on all sides. Remove to plate. Add wine, lemon juice and garlic to pot; cook and stir 1 minute, scraping up browned bits from bottom of pot. Add grapes, apricots and prunes; mix well. Return pork to pot.

3. Secure lid and move pressure release valve to Sealing position. Press Pressure Cook or Manual; cook at high pressure 20 minutes.

4. When cooking is complete, use natural release. Remove pork to cutting board; tent with foil and let stand 10 minutes.

5. Meanwhile, press Sauté; cook 10 minutes or until sauce is reduced and thickens slightly. Slice pork; serve with sauce.

Instant Pot®

WEEKNIGHT WONDERS

BBQ Chicken Sandwiches

MAKES 4 SERVINGS

- **2 pounds boneless skinless chicken thighs**
- **1 small red onion, cut in half and cut into ¼-inch slices**
- **½ cup plus 2 tablespoons barbecue sauce, divided**
- **2 tablespoons water**
- **2 tablespoons Worcestershire sauce**
- **4 pretzel rolls or sandwich buns, split**
- **½ cup cabbage slaw**

1. Combine chicken, onion, ½ cup barbecue sauce, water and Worcestershire sauce in Instant Pot; mix well. Secure lid and move pressure release valve to Sealing position. Press Pressure Cook or Manual; cook at high pressure 9 minutes.

2. When cooking is complete, use natural release for 5 minutes, then release remaining pressure. Remove chicken to bowl; let stand until cool enough to handle.

3. Meanwhile, press Sauté; cook 5 minutes or until sauce thickens slightly, stirring occasionally. Shred chicken into bite-size pieces; return to pot with remaining 2 tablespoons barbecue sauce. Cook and stir until chicken is coated.

4. Serve chicken mixture on buns with cabbage slaw.

Salsa Verde Chicken Stew

MAKES 4 TO 6 SERVINGS

- **2 cans (about 15 ounces each) black beans, rinsed and drained**
- **1½ pounds boneless skinless chicken breasts, cut into 1-inch pieces**
- **1 jar (16 ounces) salsa verde**
- **1½ cups frozen corn**
- **¾ cup chopped fresh cilantro**
- **Diced avocado (optional)**

1. Combine beans, chicken and salsa in Instant Pot; mix well.

2. Secure lid and move pressure release valve to Sealing position. Press Pressure Cook or Manual; cook at high pressure 4 minutes.

3. When cooking is complete, use quick release. Press Sauté; add corn to pot. Cook about 3 minutes or until heated through. Stir in cilantro; mix well. Garnish with avocado.

Tavern Burger

MAKES 6 SERVINGS

- 2 pounds ground beef
- ½ teaspoon salt
- ⅛ teaspoon black pepper
- ½ cup water
- ½ cup ketchup
- ¼ cup yellow mustard
- ¼ cup packed brown sugar
- 6 hamburger buns

1. Press Sauté; add beef to Instant Pot. Cook about 5 minutes or until browned, stirring to break up meat. Drain fat. Season with salt and pepper. Stir in water, ketchup, mustard and brown sugar; mix well.

2. Secure lid and move pressure release valve to Sealing position. Press Pressure Cook or Manual; cook at high pressure 5 minutes.

3. When cooking is complete, use natural release for 5 minutes, then release remaining pressure. Serve on buns.

Instant Spaghetti and Meatballs

MAKES 6 SERVINGS

- 1 pound frozen meatballs
- 8 ounces uncooked spaghetti, broken in half
- 1 tablespoon olive oil
- 3/4 teaspoon salt
- 2 cups water
- 1 jar (24 ounces) chunky marinara sauce
- Grated Parmesan cheese and fresh basil leaves (optional)

1. Place meatballs in Instant Pot in single layer. Arrange pasta in criss-crossing layers over meatballs; drizzle with oil.

2. Stir salt into water in measuring cup. Pour marinara sauce and water over pasta, making sure to cover pasta completely. (Do not stir.)

3. Secure lid and move pressure release valve to Sealing position. Press Pressure Cook or Manual; cook at high pressure 9 minutes.

4. When cooking is complete, use quick release. Gently stir with tongs to separate pasta and blend with sauce. Garnish with cheese and basil.

Chunky Black Bean and Sweet Potato Chili

MAKES 4 TO 6 SERVINGS

- 2 teaspoons vegetable oil
- 1 cup chopped sweet onion
- 2 red or green bell peppers or 1 of each, cut into ½-inch pieces
- 4 cloves garlic, minced
- 1½ teaspoons chili powder
- 1 can (about 15 ounces) black beans, rinsed and drained
- 1 can (about 14 ounces) fire-roasted diced tomatoes
- 1 medium sweet potato (12 ounces), peeled and cut into ½-inch pieces (about 2 cups)
- ⅔ cup vegetable broth or water
- 1 tablespoon minced canned chipotle peppers in adobo sauce
- 1¼ teaspoons salt
- ½ cup chopped fresh cilantro (optional)

1. Press Sauté; heat oil in Instant Pot. Add onion; cook and stir 5 minutes. Add bell peppers, garlic and chili powder; cook and stir 2 minutes. Add beans, tomatoes, sweet potato, broth, chipotle peppers and salt; mix well.

2. Secure lid and move pressure release valve to Sealing position. Press Pressure Cook or Manual; cook at high pressure 3 minutes.

3. When cooking is complete, use quick release. Stir chili; if there is excess liquid, press Sauté and cook 2 to 3 minutes or until chili thickens. Top with cilantro, if desired.

Chicken Adobo

MAKES 4 SERVINGS

- ⅓ cup cider vinegar
- ⅓ cup reduced-sodium soy sauce
- 5 cloves garlic, minced
- 3 bay leaves
- 1 teaspoon black pepper
- 2½ pounds bone-in skin-on chicken thighs
- Hot cooked rice (optional)
- Sliced green onion (optional)

1. Combine vinegar, soy sauce, garlic, bay leaves and pepper in Instant Pot; mix well. Add chicken; turn to coat. Arrange chicken skin side down in liquid.

2. Secure lid and move pressure release valve to Sealing position. Press Pressure Cook or Manual; cook at high pressure 13 minutes. Preheat broiler. Line baking sheet with foil.

3. When cooking is complete, use natural release for 10 minutes, then release remaining pressure. Remove chicken to prepared baking sheet, skin side up.

4. Broil about 4 minutes or until skin is browned and crisp. Meanwhile, press Sauté; cook liquid in pot about 5 minutes or until slightly reduced. Serve sauce over chicken and rice, if desired. Garnish with green onion.

Chorizo Burritos

MAKES 4 SERVINGS

- 14 ounces uncooked Mexican chorizo sausages, cut into bite-size pieces
- 2 green or red bell peppers, cut into 1-inch pieces
- 1 can (about 15 ounces) kidney or pinto beans, rinsed and drained
- 1 can (about 14 ounces) diced tomatoes
- 1 can (11 ounces) corn, drained
- ½ teaspoon ground cumin
- ½ teaspoon ground cinnamon
- 8 (8-inch) flour tortillas, warmed
- 2 cups hot cooked rice
- 1 cup (4 ounces) shredded Monterey Jack cheese

1. Combine chorizo, bell peppers, beans, tomatoes, corn, cumin and cinnamon in Instant Pot; mix well.

2. Secure lid and move pressure release valve to Sealing position. Press Pressure Cook or Manual; cook at high pressure 10 minutes.

3. When cooking is complete, use natural release for 10 minutes, then release remaining pressure. Press Sauté; cook about 5 minutes or until chorizo mixture thickens, stirring occasionally.

4. Spoon chorizo mixture down centers of tortillas; top with rice and cheese. Roll up tortillas; serve immediately.

One-Pot Chinese Chicken Soup

MAKES 4 SERVINGS

- 1 container (32 ounces) chicken broth
- ⅓ cup reduced-sodium soy sauce
- 1 pound boneless skinless chicken thighs
- 1 package (16 ounces) frozen stir-fry vegetables (do not thaw)
- 6 ounces uncooked thin Chinese egg noodles
- 1 to 3 tablespoons sriracha sauce

1. Combine broth and soy sauce in Instant Pot; mix well. Add chicken. Secure lid and move pressure release valve to Sealing position. Press Pressure Cook or Manual; cook at high pressure 8 minutes.

2. When cooking is complete, use quick release. Remove chicken to bowl; set aside 5 minutes or until cool enough to handle. Shred chicken into bite-size pieces.

3. Press Sauté; add vegetables and noodles to broth mixture in pot. Cook about 3 minutes or until noodles are tender. Stir in chicken and 1 tablespoon sriracha sauce; taste and add additional sauce for a spicier flavor.

Penne with Ricotta, Tomatoes and Basil

MAKES 4 SERVINGS

- 2 cans (about 14 ounces each) diced tomatoes with basil, garlic and oregano
- 2½ cups water
- 3 teaspoons salt, divided
- 1 package (16 ounces) uncooked penne pasta
- 1 container (15 ounces) ricotta cheese
- ⅔ cup chopped fresh basil
- ¼ cup extra virgin olive oil
- 1 tablespoon balsamic vinegar
- 1 clove garlic, minced
- ¼ teaspoon black pepper
- Grated Parmesan cheese

1. Combine tomatoes, water and 2 teaspoons salt in Instant Pot; mix well. Stir in pasta.

2. Secure lid and move pressure release valve to Sealing position. Press Pressure Cook or Manual; cook at high pressure 5 minutes.

3. Meanwhile, combine ricotta, basil, oil, vinegar, garlic, remaining 1 teaspoon salt and pepper in medium bowl; mix well.

4. When cooking is complete, use quick release. Drain any remaining liquid in pot. Add ricotta mixture to pot; stir gently to coat. Sprinkle with Parmesan just before serving.

Black and White Chili

MAKES 4 SERVINGS

- 1 tablespoon vegetable oil
- 1 pound chicken tenders, cut into ¾-inch pieces
- 1 cup coarsely chopped onion
- 1 can (about 14 ounces) fire-roasted diced tomatoes
- 1 can (about 15 ounces) Great Northern beans, rinsed and drained
- 1 can (about 15 ounces) black beans, rinsed and drained
- 2 tablespoons chili seasoning mix
- ¾ teaspoon salt
- Hot pepper sauce (optional)

1. Press Sauté; heat oil in Instant Pot. Add chicken and onion; cook and stir 5 minutes or until chicken begins to brown. Stir in tomatoes; cook 1 minute, scraping up browned bits from bottom of pot. Stir in beans, chili seasoning mix and salt; mix well.

2. Secure lid and move pressure release valve to Sealing position. Press Pressure Cook or Manual; cook at high pressure 5 minutes.

3. When cooking is complete, use natural release for 10 minutes, then release remaining pressure. Serve with hot pepper sauce, if desired.

Tuesday Night Tacos

MAKES 4 TO 6 SERVINGS

- 1 tablespoon vegetable oil
- 1½ pounds boneless skinless chicken thighs
- 1 cup chunky salsa
- Corn tortillas, warmed
- ½ cup shredded lettuce
- 1 cup pico de gallo
- 1 cup (4 ounces) shredded taco blend or Cheddar cheese
- Optional toppings: sour cream, sliced jalapeño peppers, pickled onions, fresh cilantro leaves, diced avocado and/or lime wedges

1. Press Sauté; heat oil in Instant Pot. Add chicken; cook 5 minutes or until browned on both sides. Add salsa; cook 1 minute, scraping up browned bits from bottom of pot. Turn chicken to coat with salsa.

2. Secure lid and move pressure release valve to Sealing position. Press Pressure Cook or Manual; cook at high pressure 11 minutes.

3. When cooking is complete, use quick release. Let stand 5 minutes, then use two forks or tongs to shred chicken into bite-size pieces in pot.

4. Serve chicken mixture in tortillas with lettuce, pico de gallo, cheese and lime wedges, if desired. Top as desired.

Instant Pot DESSERTS

Big Chocolate Chip Cookie

MAKES 6 TO 8 SERVINGS

- **1 cup plus 2 tablespoons all-purpose flour**
- **½ teaspoon baking soda**
- **½ teaspoon salt**
- **¼ cup (½ stick) butter, softened**
- **½ cup packed brown sugar**
- **2 tablespoons granulated sugar**
- **1 egg**
- **½ teaspoon vanilla**
- **1 cup semisweet chocolate chunks or chips**
- **1 cup water**

1. Spray 7-inch metal cake pan with nonstick cooking spray. Combine flour, baking soda and salt in small bowl; mix well.

2. Beat butter, brown sugar and granulated sugar in medium bowl with electric mixer at medium speed until light and creamy. Add egg and vanilla; beat until well blended. Add flour mixture; beat just until blended. Stir in chocolate chunks. Spread batter in prepared pan. Cover pan with paper towel (to absorb moisture), making sure paper towel does not touch batter. Cover pan with foil over paper towel.

3. Pour water into Instant Pot; place rack in pot. Place pan on rack. Secure lid and move pressure release valve to Sealing position. Press Pressure Cook or Manual; cook at high pressure 35 minutes.

4. When cooking is complete, use natural release for 10 minutes, then release remaining pressure. Remove pan from pot. Uncover; cool on wire rack 15 minutes. Invert cookie onto plate; invert again onto serving plate. Serve warm or at room temperature.

Pumpkin Pie

MAKES 8 SERVINGS

- 1½ cups graham cracker crumbs
- 2 tablespoons granulated sugar
- ¼ cup (½ stick) butter, melted
- 1 can (15 ounces) pure pumpkin
- ½ cup evaporated milk
- 2 eggs
- ½ cup packed brown sugar
- 2 teaspoons pumpkin pie spice
- 1 teaspoon vanilla
- ½ teaspoon salt
- 1 cup water
- Whipped cream (optional)

1. Spray 7-inch springform pan with nonstick cooking spray. Combine graham cracker crumbs and granulated sugar in small bowl; mix well. Stir in butter until well blended. Use bottom of glass or measuring cup to press mixture evenly into bottom and 1 inch up side of prepared pan. Freeze crust 10 minutes while preparing filling.

2. Beat pumpkin, evaporated milk, eggs, brown sugar, pumpkin pie spice, vanilla and salt in medium bowl until smooth and well blended. Wrap bottom of springform pan with foil. Pour filling into crust. Cover pan with foil.

3. Pour water into Instant Pot; place rack in pot. Place pan on rack. Secure lid and move pressure release valve to Sealing position. Press Pressure Cook or Manual; cook at high pressure 40 minutes.

4. When cooking is complete, use natural release for 10 minutes, then release remaining pressure. Remove pan from pot. Uncover; cool on wire rack 1 hour. Refrigerate overnight before sliding knife around edge and removing side of pan. Serve with whipped cream, if desired.

Chocolate Bundt Cake

MAKES 8 SERVINGS

- 3/4 cup boiling water
- 1/2 cup unsweetened cocoa powder
- 1/2 teaspoon espresso powder or instant coffee granules
- 1 1/4 cups all-purpose flour
- 1 teaspoon baking soda
- 1/2 teaspoon salt
- 1/4 teaspoon baking powder
- 1 1/4 cups sugar
- 2 eggs
- 1/2 teaspoon vanilla
- 1/2 cup vegetable oil
- 1/3 cup sour cream
- 1 1/2 cups water
- 1/4 cup whipping cream
- 1/2 cup bittersweet or semisweet chocolate chips

1. Spray 6-cup bundt pan with nonstick cooking spray. Combine 3/4 cup boiling water, cocoa and espresso powder in small bowl or measuring cup; whisk until smooth. Set aside to cool slightly.

2. Combine flour, baking soda, salt and baking powder in medium bowl; mix well. Beat sugar, eggs and vanilla in large bowl until well blended. Stir in oil and sour cream; mix well. Add flour mixture; stir until blended. Add cocoa mixture; stir just until blended. Pour batter into prepared pan; cover with foil.

3. Pour 1 1/2 cups water into Instant Pot; place rack in pot. Place pan on rack. Secure lid and move pressure release valve to Sealing position. Press Pressure Cook or Manual; cook at high pressure 27 minutes.

4. When cooking is complete, use natural release for 10 minutes, then release remaining pressure. Remove pan from pot. Uncover; let stand 10 minutes. Invert cake onto serving plate; cool completely.

5. Heat cream to a simmer in microwave oven or in small saucepan over low heat. Add chocolate chips; stir until melted and smooth. Drizzle glaze over cake.

Perfect Cheesecake

MAKES 8 SERVINGS

- ½ cup graham cracker crumbs
- ½ cup plus 1 tablespoon sugar, divided
- 2 tablespoons butter, melted
- 2 packages (8 ounces each) cream cheese, softened
- 2 eggs, at room temperature
- 1 teaspoon vanilla
- 1½ cups water

1. Cut parchment paper to fit bottom of 7-inch springform pan. Lightly spray bottom and side of pan with nonstick cooking spray. Wrap outside of pan with foil.

2. Combine graham cracker crumbs, 1 tablespoon sugar and melted butter in small bowl; mix well. Pat mixture into bottom of prepared pan. Freeze crust 10 minutes while preparing filling.

3. Beat cream cheese in large bowl with electric mixer at medium-high speed until smooth and creamy. Add remaining ½ cup sugar; beat about 3 minutes or until light and fluffy. Add eggs, one at a time, beating well after each addition. Stir in vanilla. Pour batter into prepared crust. Cover pan with foil.

4. Pour water into Instant Pot; place rack in pot. Place pan on rack. Secure lid and move pressure release valve to Sealing position. Press Pressure Cook or Manual; cook at high pressure 33 minutes.

5. When cooking is complete, use quick release. Remove pan from pot. Uncover; cool on wire rack 1 hour. Run thin knife around edge of cheesecake to loosen (do not remove side of pan). Refrigerate 2 to 3 hours or overnight.

Peanut Butter Pie

MAKES 8 SERVINGS

- 10 cream-filled chocolate sandwich cookies, crushed into fine crumbs
- 1½ tablespoons butter, melted
- ⅔ cup creamy peanut butter
- ½ cup plus 2 tablespoons whipping cream, divided
- 2 eggs
- ⅓ cup whole milk
- ¼ cup packed brown sugar
- ½ teaspoon salt
- ½ teaspoon vanilla
- ⅓ cup plus ¼ cup semisweet chocolate chips, divided
- 1½ cups water
- 2 to 3 tablespoons chopped roasted salted peanuts

1. Spray 7-inch springform pan with nonstick cooking spray. Combine cookie crumbs and butter in small bowl; mix well. Use bottom of glass or measuring cup to press mixture evenly into bottom of prepared pan. Freeze crust 10 minutes while preparing filling.

2. Whisk peanut butter, ½ cup cream, eggs, milk, brown sugar, salt and vanilla in medium bowl until well blended. Sprinkle ⅓ cup chocolate chips over bottom of crust. Pour peanut butter mixture over chocolate chips. Cover pan with foil.

3. Pour water into Instant Pot; place rack in pot. Place pan on rack. Secure lid and move pressure release valve to Sealing position. Press Pressure Cook or Manual; cook at high pressure 34 minutes.

4. When cooking is complete, use natural release for 10 minutes, then release remaining pressure. Remove pan from pot. Uncover; cool to room temperature. Cover and refrigerate at least 4 hours or overnight.

5. Heat remaining 2 tablespoons cream to a simmer in microwave oven or in small saucepan over low heat. Add remaining ¼ cup chocolate chips; stir until chocolate is melted and mixture is smooth. Remove side of pan. Sprinkle peanuts over pie; drizzle with chocolate glaze.

Carrot Cake

MAKES 8 SERVINGS

- 1 cup all-purpose flour
- 1 teaspoon baking soda
- 1 teaspoon ground cinnamon
- 1/4 teaspoon salt
- 2/3 cup granulated sugar
- 1/2 cup vegetable oil
- 2 eggs
- 1 teaspoon vanilla
- 1 1/2 cups grated carrots (about 3 medium)
- 1/2 cup chopped walnuts or pecans
- 1 1/2 cups water
- 2 ounces cream cheese, softened
- 1/4 cup powdered sugar
- 2 to 3 tablespoons milk

1. Spray 6-cup bundt pan with nonstick cooking spray. Combine flour, baking soda, cinnamon and salt in small bowl; mix well.

2. Beat granulated sugar, oil, eggs and vanilla in medium bowl until well blended. Add flour mixture; stir just until blended. Add carrots and walnuts; stir until blended. Pour batter into prepared pan; cover with foil.

3. Pour water into Instant Pot; place rack in pot. Place pan on rack. Secure lid and move pressure release valve to Sealing position. Press Pressure Cook or Manual; cook at high pressure 37 minutes.

4. When cooking is complete, use natural release for 10 minutes, then release remaining pressure. Remove pan from pot. Uncover; let stand 10 minutes. Invert cake onto serving plate; cool completely.

5. Beat cream cheese in small bowl until smooth. (A hand mixer is best as quantities are too small for most stand mixers.) Add powdered sugar; beat until smooth. Beat in 2 tablespoons milk until blended. Add additional milk, 1 teaspoon at a time, if necessary to reach desired consistency. Drizzle glaze over cake. Let stand until set.

Peach Melba Dump Cake

MAKES 6 SERVINGS

- 1 can (21 ounces) peach pie filling
- 1 package (12 ounces) frozen raspberries, thawed and drained
- ½ (15-ounce) package yellow cake mix
- ¼ cup (½ stick) butter, cut into thin slices
- 1 cup water
- Ice cream (optional)

1. Spray 1½-quart (6- to 7-inch) soufflé dish with nonstick cooking spray. Pour pie filling into soufflé dish; top with raspberries. Spread dry cake mix over fruit; top with butter in single layer, covering cake mix as much as possible. Cover dish with foil.

2. Pour water into Instant Pot. Place rack in pot; place soufflé dish on rack. Secure lid and move pressure release valve to Sealing position. Press Pressure Cook or Manual; cook at high pressure 40 minutes. Preheat broiler.

3. When cooking is complete, use natural release for 10 minutes, then release remaining pressure. Uncover; remove soufflé dish from pot. Broil 6 to 8 inches from heat source 4 minutes or until top is golden brown. Cool at least 15 minutes before serving. Top with ice cream, if desired.

Classic Rice Pudding

MAKES 4 SERVINGS

- 1 cup uncooked long grain rice
- 1½ cups water
- ¼ cup raisins
- 1 teaspoon salt
- 1 cinnamon stick (optional)
- 2 eggs
- ½ cup sugar
- 2 cups milk
- 1 teaspoon vanilla

1. Combine rice, water, raisins, salt and cinnamon stick, if desired, in Instant Pot; mix well. Secure lid and move pressure release valve to Sealing position. Press Pressure Cook or Manual; cook at high pressure 7 minutes.

2. When cooking is complete, use quick release. Remove and discard cinnamon stick. Whisk eggs and sugar in medium bowl 1 minute. Whisk in milk and vanilla until well blended. Press Sauté; slowly add milk mixture to pot, stirring constantly.

3. Cook 5 minutes or until pudding thickens, stirring frequently. Serve warm or chilled. (Pudding will also thicken as it cools.)

Sunshine Lemon Pie

MAKES 8 SERVINGS

- 1 cup graham cracker crumbs
- 1 tablespoon sugar
- 2 tablespoons butter, melted
- 4 egg yolks
- 1 can (14 ounces) sweetened condensed milk
- 1/3 cup lemon juice
- 1/4 cup sour cream
- 1½ tablespoons grated lemon peel, plus additional for garnish
- 1 cup water
- Whipped cream (optional)
- Fresh blueberries (optional)

1. Spray 7-inch springform pan with nonstick cooking spray. Combine graham cracker crumbs and sugar in small bowl; mix well. Stir in butter until well blended. Use bottom of glass or measuring cup to press mixture evenly into bottom of prepared pan. Freeze crust 10 minutes while preparing filling.

2. Beat egg yolks in large bowl until lightened in color. Slowly add sweetened condensed milk, beating until thickened. Add lemon juice, sour cream and 1½ tablespoons lemon peel; beat until well blended. Pour filling into crust. Cover pan with foil.

3. Pour water into Instant Pot; place rack in pot. Place pan on rack. Secure lid and move pressure release valve to Sealing position. Press Pressure Cook or Manual; cook at high pressure 20 minutes.

4. When cooking is complete, use natural release for 10 minutes, then release remaining pressure. Remove pan from pot. Uncover; blot any condensation on top of pie with paper towel, if necessary. Cool to room temperature. Cover and refrigerate at least 4 hours or overnight.

5. Remove side of pan. Garnish pie with additional lemon peel and whipped cream; serve with blueberries, if desired.

Magic Chocoflan

MAKES ABOUT 10 SERVINGS

- 1/3 cup caramel ice cream topping or caramel sauce

CAKE

- 3/4 cup all-purpose flour
- 1/4 cup unsweetened cocoa powder
- 1/2 teaspoon baking soda
- 1/2 teaspoon baking powder
- 1/2 teaspoon espresso powder
- 1/4 teaspoon salt
- 1/3 cup butter, softened
- 1/2 cup sugar
- 1 egg
- 1/2 cup buttermilk

FLAN

- 1/2 (14-ounce) can sweetened condensed milk
- 1/2 (12-ounce) can evaporated milk
- 2 eggs
- 1/2 teaspoon vanilla
- 1 1/2 cups water

1. Spray 6-cup bundt pan with nonstick cooking spray. Spread caramel topping in even layer in bottom of pan. For cake, combine flour, cocoa, baking soda, baking powder, espresso powder and salt in small bowl; mix well. Beat butter and sugar in medium bowl with electric mixer at medium speed about 3 minutes or until light and fluffy, scraping down side of bowl several times. Add 1 egg; beat until well blended. Alternately add flour mixture and buttermilk in two additions, beating just until blended. (Do not overbeat.)

2. For flan, combine sweetened condensed milk, evaporated milk, 2 eggs and vanilla in blender; blend about 1 minute or until smooth. Spoon cake batter into prepared pan over caramel layer; spread evenly and smooth top. Slowly pour flan mixture over cake batter.

3. Pour water into Instant Pot; place rack in pot. Place pan on rack. Secure lid and move pressure release valve to Sealing position. Press Pressure Cook or Manual; cook at high pressure 17 minutes.

4. When cooking is complete, use natural release for 15 minutes, then release remaining pressure. Remove pan from pot; cool to room temperature on wire rack.

5. Place serving plate over pan; invert chocoflan onto plate. Scrape any caramel left in pan onto top of chocoflan.

Choco-Toffee Pudding Cake

MAKES 6 TO 8 SERVINGS

- **1 cup all-purpose flour**
- **½ cup packed brown sugar**
- **5 tablespoons unsweetened cocoa powder, divided**
- **1½ teaspoons baking powder**
- **½ teaspoon salt**
- **½ cup milk**
- **¼ cup (½ stick) butter, melted**
- **½ teaspoon vanilla**
- **½ cup milk chocolate toffee bits**
- **½ cup semisweet chocolate chips**
- **⅓ cup granulated sugar**
- **1 cup boiling water**
- **1 cup water**
- **Vanilla ice cream (optional)**

1. Spray 1½-quart (6- to 7-inch) soufflé dish with nonstick cooking spray.

2. Combine flour, brown sugar, 3 tablespoons cocoa, baking powder and salt in medium bowl; mix well. Add milk, butter and vanilla; stir until smooth and well blended. Stir in toffee bits and chocolate chips. Spread batter in prepared soufflé dish.

3. Combine granulated sugar and remaining 2 tablespoons cocoa in small bowl; stir in 1 cup boiling water until well blended. Pour over batter. (Do not stir.) Cover dish with foil.

4. Pour 1 cup water into Instant Pot. Place rack in pot; place soufflé dish on rack. Secure lid and move pressure release valve to Sealing position. Press Pressure Cook or Manual; cook at high pressure 33 minutes.

5. When cooking is complete, use natural release for 10 minutes, then release remaining pressure. Remove soufflé dish from pot. Uncover; cool 5 minutes before serving. Serve with ice cream, if desired.

PRESSURE COOKING TIMES

Meat

Meat	MINUTES UNDER PRESSURE	PRESSURE	RELEASE
Beef, Bone-in Short Ribs	35 to 45	High	Natural
Beef, Brisket	60 to 75	High	Natural
Beef, Ground	8	High	Natural
Beef, Roast (round, rump or shoulder)	60 to 70	High	Natural
Beef, Stew Meat	20 to 25	High	Natural or Quick
Lamb, Chops	5 to 10	High	Quick
Lamb, Leg or Shanks	35 to 40	High	Natural
Lamb, Stew Meat	12 to 15	High	Quick
Pork, Baby Back Ribs	25 to 30	High	Natural
Pork, Chops	7 to 10	High	Quick
Pork, Ground	5	High	Quick
Pork, Loin	15 to 25	High	Natural
Pork, Shoulder or Butt	45 to 60	High	Natural
Pork, Stew Meat	15 to 20	High	Quick

Poultry

Poultry	MINUTES UNDER PRESSURE	PRESSURE	RELEASE
Chicken Breasts, Bone-in	7 to 10	High	Quick
Chicken Breasts, Boneless	5 to 8	High	Quick
Chicken Thigh, Bone-in	10 to 14	High	Natural
Chicken Thigh, Boneless	8 to 10	High	Natural
Chicken Wings	10 to 12	High	Quick

Chicken, Whole	22 to 26	High	Natural
Eggs, Hard-Cooked (3 to 12)	9	Low	Quick
Turkey Breast, Bone-in	25 to 30	High	Natural
Turkey Breast, Boneless	15 to 20	High	Natural
Turkey Legs	35 to 40	High	Natural
Turkey, Ground	8 to 10	High	Quick

Seafood

	MINUTES UNDER PRESSURE	PRESSURE	RELEASE
Cod	2 to 3	Low	Quick
Crab	2 to 3	Low	Quick
Halibut	6	Low	Quick
Mussels	1 to 2	Low	Quick
Salmon	4 to 5	Low	Quick
Scallops	1	Low	Quick
Shrimp	2 to 3	Low	Quick
Swordfish	4 to 5	Low	Quick
Tilapia	3	Low	Quick

Dried Beans and Legumes

	UNSOAKED	SOAKED	PRESSURE	RELEASE
Black Beans	22 to 25	8 to 10	High	Natural
Black-Eyed Peas	9 to 11	3 to 5	High	Natural
Cannellini Beans	30 to 35	8 to 10	High	Natural
Chickpeas	35 to 40	18 to 22	High	Natural
Great Northern Beans	25 to 30	7 to 10	High	Natural

Kidney Beans	20 to 25	8 to 12	High	Natural
Lentils, Brown or Green	10 to 12	n/a	High	Natural
Lentils, Red or Yellow Split	1	n/a	High	Natural
Navy Beans	20 to 25	7 to 8	High	Natural
Pinto Beans	22 to 25	8 to 10	High	Natural
Split Peas	8 to 10	n/a	High	Natural

Grains	LIQUID PER CUP	MINUTES UNDER PRESSURE	PRESSURE	RELEASE
Barley, Pearl	2	18 to 22	High	Natural
Barley, Whole	2½	30 to 35	High	Natural
Bulgur	3	8	High	Natural
Farro	2	10 to 12	High	Natural
Grits, Medium	4	12 to 15	High	10 minute natural
Millet	1½	1	High	Natural
Oats, Rolled	2	4 to 5	High	10 minute natural
Oats, Steel-Cut	3	10 to 13	High	10 minute natural
Quinoa	1½	1	High	10 minute natural
Polenta, Instant	3	5	High	5 minute natural
Rice, Arborio	2	6 to 7	High	Quick
Rice, Brown	1	22	High	10 minute natural
Rice, White Long Grain	1	4	High	10 minute natural

Vegetables	MINUTES UNDER PRESSURE	PRESSURE	RELEASE
Artichokes, Whole	9 to 12	High	Natural
Beets, Medium Whole	18 to 24	High	Quick
Brussels Sprouts, Whole	2 to 3	High	Quick

Cabbage, Sliced	3 to 5	High	Quick
Carrots, Sliced	2 to 4	High	Quick
Cauliflower, Florets	2 to 3	High	Quick
Cauliflower, Whole	3 to 5	High	Quick
Corn on the Cob	2 to 4	High	Quick
Eggplant	3 to 4	High	Quick
Fennel, Sliced	3 to 4	High	Quick
Green Beans	2 to 4	High	Quick
Kale	3	High	Quick
Leeks	3	High	Quick
Okra	3	High	Quick
Potatoes, Baby or Fingerling	6 to 10	High	Natural
Potatoes, New	7 to 9	High	Natural
Potatoes, 1-inch pieces	4 to 6	High	Quick
Potatoes, Sweet, 1-inch pieces	3	High	Quick
Potatoes, Sweet, Whole	8 to 12	High	Natural
Spinach	1	High	Quick
Squash, Acorn, Halved	7	High	Natural
Squash, Butternut, 1-inch pieces	4 to 6	High	Quick
Squash, Spaghetti, Halved	6 to 10	High	Natural
Tomatoes, cut into pieces for sauce	5	High	Natural

VOLUME MEASUREMENTS (dry)

1/8 teaspoon = 0.5 mL
1/4 teaspoon = 1 mL
1/2 teaspoon = 2 mL
3/4 teaspoon = 4 mL
1 teaspoon = 5 mL
1 tablespoon = 15 mL
2 tablespoons = 30 mL
1/4 cup = 60 mL
1/3 cup = 75 mL
1/2 cup = 125 mL
2/3 cup = 150 mL
3/4 cup = 175 mL
1 cup = 250 mL
2 cups = 1 pint = 500 mL
3 cups = 750 mL
4 cups = 1 quart = 1 L

VOLUME MEASUREMENTS (fluid)

1 fluid ounce (2 tablespoons) = 30 mL
4 fluid ounces (1/2 cup) = 125 mL
8 fluid ounces (1 cup) = 250 mL
12 fluid ounces (1 1/2 cups) = 375 mL
16 fluid ounces (2 cups) = 500 mL

WEIGHTS (mass)

1/2 ounce = 15 g
1 ounce = 30 g
3 ounces = 90 g
4 ounces = 120 g
8 ounces = 225 g
10 ounces = 285 g
12 ounces = 360 g
16 ounces = 1 pound = 450 g

DIMENSIONS

1/16 inch = 2 mm
1/8 inch = 3 mm
1/4 inch = 6 mm
1/2 inch = 1.5 cm
3/4 inch = 2 cm
1 inch = 2.5 cm

OVEN TEMPERATURES

250°F = 120°C
275°F = 140°C
300°F = 150°C
325°F = 160°C
350°F = 180°C
375°F = 190°C
400°F = 200°C
425°F = 220°C
450°F = 230°C

BAKING PAN SIZES

Utensil	Size in Inches/Quarts	Metric Volume	Size in Centimeters
Baking or Cake Pan (square or rectangular)	8×8×2	2 L	20×20×5
	9×9×2	2.5 L	23×23×5
	12×8×2	3 L	30×20×5
	13×9×2	3.5 L	33×23×5
Loaf Pan	8×4×3	1.5 L	20×10×7
	9×5×3	2 L	23×13×7
Round Layer Cake Pan	8×1½	1.2 L	20×4
	9×1½	1.5 L	23×4
Pie Plate	8×1¼	750 mL	20×3
	9×1¼	1 L	23×3
Baking Dish or Casserole	1 quart	1 L	—
	1½ quart	1.5 L	—
	2 quart	2 L	—